Endorsements for *Easy Hikes*

"Rocky and Tim have shared their many ye ___ .
Pikes Peak region in a book that visitors and residents will find valuable for
years to come."
—**Doug Price, President & CEO, Visit Colorado Springs**

"An excellent guide to explore the trails and history of the Pikes Peak
region! Each hike leads you on an adventure of discovery—sometimes
beyond the beaten path, other times just by looking a little more closely
along well-known trails and open spaces. With a blend of entertaining story,
historical insight and helpful trail detail, Rocky Shockley and T. Duren Jones
prove to be knowledgeable and enjoyable guides, whether you're new to the
Colorado Springs area or have been hiking its paths for years."
—**Jeremy Jones, Editorial Director, *Springs Magazine*/SpringsMag.com**

"A hike in the Pikes Peak Region becomes a trip through time when
accompanied on the trail with this energetic guidebook. The easy storytelling
style reads like a Wild West adventure tale told around a blazing campfire.
Loaded with sensory detail, history, scientific fact, humor, folklore and
legend, *Easy Hikes to the Hidden Past* entertains while educating readers
curious about what they'll experience along the wilderness region's
accessible trails. Practical tips shared are applicable for hikes of any distance
or difficulty. Even if you never step foot on a trail, this guide is an engaging,
insightful read for armchair travelers and active adventurers alike interested
in the Pikes Peak Region's rich history and rugged beauty."
—**Kit Bernardi, Travel Journalist & Photographer,**
   KitTravels.com & Instagram @KitBernardi

"...Colorado Springs resident Rocky Shockley has busied himself with long hours in the library and long hours on the trail, in search of history hiding in plain sight across the Pikes Peak foothills.... The result is *Easy Hikes to the Hidden Past*, written along Shockley's partner, T Duren Jones.... The guidebook includes 20 locations for exploring and pondering—for transporting back to the heydays of the cracked, crumbled and rusted relics on display along the way."
—**Seth Boster,** *The Gazette*

"It is a simple truth that the more you learn about a valued friend, the more you love them. The trails in this book, the very ones that I have been hiking for the past 35 years, are even more special to me now. They will no longer be just trails with pretty creeks and flowers, tasty berries in the summer, coyote tracks in the snow or one more cool quartz rock. Our bond goes much deeper now that we have *history* attached. Thank you Rocky and Tim for sharing your knowledge and love for this beautiful area and helping me to love it more too."
—**Sasha Burke, Manager, Seven Falls Attraction**

"I highly recommend Rocky Shockley and T. Duren Jones' book, *Easy Hikes to the Hidden Past*, to anyone interested in hiking in the Pikes Peak Region. This book makes a wonderful hiking companion, for new or experienced hikers alike, who want to have trail information available at a glance; including, an easy to read map, accompanied by a clever trail marker sign offering trail distance, elevation gain and difficulty level (measured in tree numbers!)."
—**John Wesley Anderson, former El Paso County Sheriff, Author**

Easy Hikes to the Hidden Past

Pikes Peak Region Edition

Rocky Shockley

T. Duren Jones

findusoutside@outlook.com
6100feet.com/book

NOTE: Every effort has been made by the authors to be accurate in the trail descriptions. Still, some discrepancies may exist between this guide book and actual trail directions and conditions. Before heading out for an adventure to the past, users should know that they are capable of independent wilderness hiking and exploring. Failure to be prepared with the necessary knowledge, conditioning, clothing, equipment and relevant outdoor skills could subject hikers to physical danger, injury or death. The authors have tried to help the readers with preparedness in the Appendix inserts at the end of this book and cannot be held responsible for any trail changes, hazards, weather-related issues or lack of readiness by users. Outdoor sports and adventuring have natural, inherent dangers and no guide book can substitute for good judgement. Play safe. Play smart. Do not trespass.

Cover design and site photography by T. Duren Jones
Interior design, maps and formatting by Rocky Shockley

What will you find inside this book?

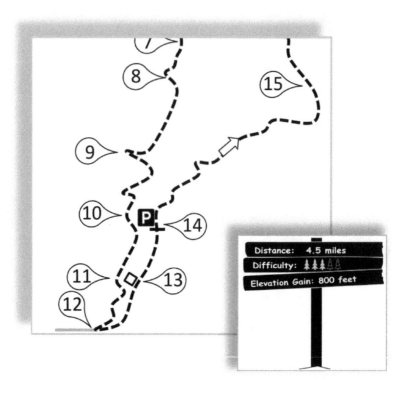

- Guided hikes with full-page maps
- Detailed trail descriptions
- A brief history of the trails and finds
- Discoveries along the way
- Anecdotal stories and experiences
- Historic and trailside photos

Chapters

Know Yourself; Know the Wilderness and the Terrain

Getting out into the wilderness and getting away from everything else has its rewards but, there is still the wilderness. There are mountain lions, bobcats and black bears. Rattlesnakes, biting bugs and Big Foot. Or not. The chance of a critter encounter on the trail—other than a squirrel or two—is slim, but it is good to keep an eye out.

The Pikes Peak Region is a dry climate with rapidly changing weather. Dehydration and fast moving thunderstorms. Lightning, hail and quick temperature swings, are not out of the question. Not enough oxygen and too much sun. You may experience bright sun, ice, mud, skree, tree roots and that pesky gravity issue. Be smart, play safe. Tell someone where you are going. See the appendix in the back for more tips.

Please use good judgment and know your capabilities before you start and along the way. It is okay to turn around. Another adventure awaits another day.

Stories and Sources

In the back of this book you will find some hints on doing your own history hiking research. Some of our sources are tales and memories from locals and old timers. Even in the historical archives the facts can differ. Embellishment is not uncommon in the old texts. If the stories differ, our choice was easy: the most entertaining facts were chosen.

There are countless beautiful trails in the region and there are pioneer artifacts galore. These chapters are about the trails that combine both. Enjoy.

MANITOU SPRINGS

It is by design that the first five chapters in the book originate in and around Manitou Springs. Situated at the mouth of Ute Pass, this little mountain town is a perfect combination of the two themes that we sought to combine, a nice hike and mankind's early mark on the area.

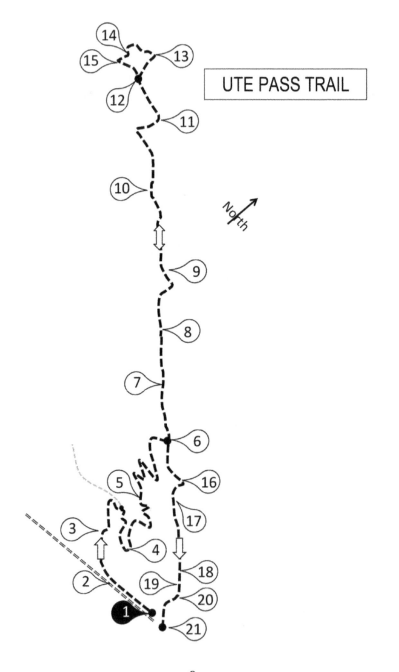

UTE PASS TRAIL

North

1
Ute Pass Trail
Walking the original path

Forest animals create the most pragmatic trails to food, water, shelter. Man follows. Ancient travelers, followed by the Ute Indians, then homesteaders and prospectors, used this valley to pass between the plains and mountains. Wagons and then automobiles lumbered up the canyon. Intriguing train tunnels smoked from steam engines of the past. It's the same story all over the country. What makes this stretch surprisingly different is that the Ute Trail still exists because the modern version was built in the valley below the original trail, leaving the original trail in place. Somewhat isolated with good elevation gains, this trail still has a story to tell.

Evidence shows that this is one of the earliest migration routes known in the United States. Approximately 10,000 years ago it was a vital gap to approach the mountains beyond, and it still is. If you view this pass on a topographical map it is easy to see why this little valley was so valuable.

Ute Pass is now a gateway to the Rocky Mountains for the camping, four-wheeling, hiking, skiing and biking adventurers of the region. It hosts a steady stream of smiles, bumper stickers, roof top car carriers, happy dogs and mountain toys that are heading for the hills. Driving through scenic Manitou

Springs and Woodland Park is an easy way to get into the mountain frame of mind at the start of the journey.

Getting there: From the town of Manitou Springs, just west of Downtown Colorado Springs, take the free shuttle to the top of Ruxton Avenue. From the bus stop **(1)**, head uphill and bear to the right to get to the base **(2)** of the Mount Manitou Incline.

The hike: While most people are going up the steps, you start your journey by bearing right on the gravel trail. Here you will spot the first of several informational signs about the route. It gives us pause to read that there are records of this pass being used in 1779.

After the sign, is it entertaining to note how the trail parallels the Incline for a short distance and the gives a unique view looking up at the wooden railway tie steps from below. Soon you will encounter a large diameter pipeline **(3)** that brings the water from the reservoirs that are adjacent to the Pikes Peak Highway.

After the first major switchback in the trail, you will encounter an intersection with the Northern Incline Trail, a return route for the incline hikers. For safety reasons, the incline it is one-way uphill. Routing the downhill half of the hike to this piece of Ute Pass Trail thankfully takes the load off of Barr Trail. You will find that the downhill traffic on the Ute Pass Trail decreases dramatically after passing this connection. (At this time, the trail intersects the incline at roughly the mid-point. It will continue to the top of the incline in the near future.)

As you gain elevation the big views appear. Below you are the Pikes Peak Cog Train facilities. The brick building for the hydroelectric generation station can also be seen. The Incline is still visible, but the attention is now being drawn by the expansive views below. Continue to climb to the first big sweeping turn in the trail **(4)**. A view to remember awaits you. Now is not the time to hurry on.

Remnants of a small stone building

Near the top of the climb, you will spot some remnants of a building. The stone walls of a small and very short building **(5)** remains. As little as a few years ago, this building had a roof and wire fence attached for an animal pen. The only other structure up here at the time was the weathered fallen poles of a teepee, still lashed together. All of that is now gone, but the stone walls remain. Due to the small size, we'd like to think it was a sheep pen or similar stock that had a wonderful view of the town below.

11

A bit farther on you will descend from this high point but you will soon be gaining elevation again. This trail intersects a utility road **(6)** that is access for the pipeline, water tank and pumping station. When you encounter the junction, turn left. (On the return trip, you will be going straight down past the water tank towards Rattlesnake Gulch.) Along this portion of the trail, there is an assortment of weathered iron signs that have been here for a very long time. The 7000' CASCADE 2 MI sign **(7)** is the first of several you will spot. Just a few years ago, I explored this trail when it was an almost forgotten path. These signs were exciting finds in the bushes along the trek. Fortunately, the city made the effort to upgrade the Ute Pass Trail to what you see today. The modern signs are very informative and enhance the hike, but there is something about the rusty, bent signs that really make it feel like an exploration.

The next sign **(8)** is a favorite, not only for what it announces, but because it has an exclamation mark: "This point marks original intersection of Ute Trail and Ute Wagon Trail!" It looks like a great deal of labor went into stenciling the words then cutting it out with a torch, but they have lasted many times longer than any modern sign could. Standing at this sign facing downhill, you will see there is a little gully with the faintest hint of a road. This is the wagon road that starts at Rainbow Falls in Manitou Springs. It is so overgrown and eroded that one could easily walk right by this important piece of history. This road was replaced in 1872 by a road that parallels the river in the valley below that later became the route for Highway 24. Thankfully this old sign with the exclamation point has kept us from missing this historic junction.

As you descend from the summit of this trail **(9)** you will pass under a large diameter water pipe that crosses high overhead on a trestle **(10)** built in the 1930s. This spot was the site of Longs Ranch. Vegetables and non-native plants can still be found growing in this area from the family's gardens. A modern interpretive sign at this location tells the story.

Continuing on down the trial, a sign from the past **(11)** states that this is the UPT. This rusty old sign appears to have arrows on either end giving the impression that a trail may have joined here in the past.

Pipeline trestle over the Ute Pass Trail

Have you noticed that Highway 24 has not been seen? Considering the fact that this trail parallels the busy east-west highway in the valley below, it is surprising that the road has not been seen the entire time. Even more surprising is that the traffic noise is not intruding on the peaceful hike.

The trail now splits **(12)** into a loop. Take this loop counterclockwise by going to the right. You will quickly reach an informative kiosk **(13)** and then loop around to return to this point. The dirt road you cross continues on but it is not recommended to go any farther at this time. Plans are to have this trail continue on to Cascade and beyond as a vital link of the Ring The Peak Trail.

After the kiosk, follow the loop around until you find the water pipeline **(14)** running into a tunnel. There are nine tunnels along this line, just big enough for the pipe to pass under a ridge. Finding these little discoveries are the rewards for getting out to explore.

"This red earth is the dust of my grandfather's bones..." It is time for a treat and a pause for thought **(15)** at the medicine wheel that was placed during the trail's dedication. More information can be found in **A Step Farther** at the end of this chapter.

Retrace your steps down this trail. When you come to the point that you dropped down to join this trail **(6)**, continue straight ahead. You will pass the town's waterworks and storage tank **(16)**.

The descent gets steeper **(17)**. It is hard to picture this steep hill as the start of the original trail; it must have been quite a haul. At one time there was a road straight up this little valley as witnessed by the wide iron gate **(18)** that once blocked the old road that still has a welded "Foot Traffic Only" sign on the crossbar. One hundred and fifty years of erosion makes it hard to tell where the original trail was located. There is a trail that is a bit more gentle **(19)** that cuts off to the left, but stay on the trail that goes straight down the hill. There is an interpretative sign nearby that states this is one of the oldest known routes in the United States. It also emphasizes "Caution Steep Trail Ahead" for good reason. Heed that warning because skree tends to roll underfoot. At the base of the hill, the trail curves to your right. Look for the rusty iron Rattlesnake Gulch sign that is quite old **(20)**. This colorful name sounds as if it comes from an old Western novel.

The trail snakes behind some townhomes and past an old pulley wheel from the Manitou Incline's cable car days **(21)** ending at the parking lot across from the Cog Railway. Now, it is a simple matter of hopping on the free shuttle bus to return to your vehicle. Or better yet, walk down Ruxton Avenue to a celebratory meal in town. Enjoy, you've earned it.—RS

Rattlesnake Gulch Sign

A Step Farther:
Wheel in the sky

The Medicine Wheel, also known as the Sacred Hoop, has been used by generations of Native Americans to support their belief that it served the tribe for health and healing. The Medicine Wheel can be thought of as a metaphor for a variety of spiritual concepts and often takes different forms. It can be artwork like a painting, or it can be a physical construction on the land with the use of stones. Thousands of these symbols have been built across North America on native lands over several centuries.

It has been said that when strangers from different tribes met, they would ask each other, "What land do you belong to?" They felt they belonged to the land where they lived, not the other way around. At each encampment, the Medicine Man or Woman would build a Four Directions symbol, with a Heart Stone at the center.

In this chapter, you encounter a Medicine Wheel. Visitors are asked not to disturb it out of respect. When you hike the Iron Mountain chapter, you will encounter a similar wheel, except you are actually encouraged to add to this medicine wheel.

In your wanderings above Manitou Springs you may see trinket offerings hanging in trees, Tibetan prayer flags or maybe some mysterious stone circles built in areas away from the trail. The Ute Pass medicine wheel is just one small piece that makes Manitou Springs such a special town.—TDJ

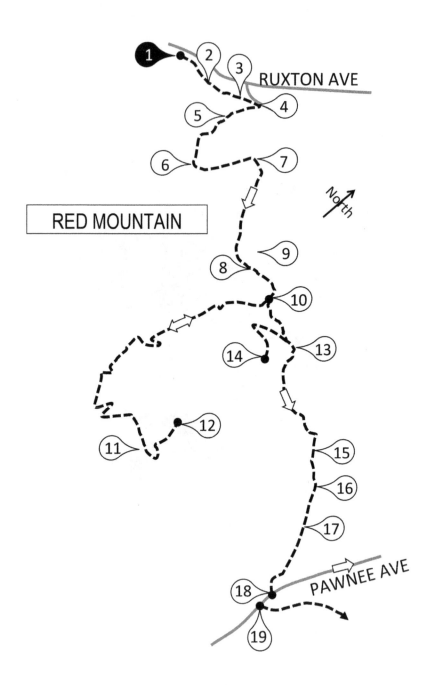

RUXTON AVE

RED MOUNTAIN

North

PAWNEE AVE

2

Red Mountain

The forgotten funicular

If one is good, two are better. The Mount Manitou Incline was such a hit with the tourists that competition for the tourist dollar was sure to be built. While the main funicular has lived on to become the wonderfully torturous Mount Manitou Incline hike, the smaller Red Mountain Incline faded off into obscurity. Fortunately there are some remnants of the buildings that are still on top that can be explored with a short hike. We suggest some lightweight binoculars with you as the view from up there will be memorable. You will be returning down Pawnee Avenue and coming out where it intersects Manitou Avenue and an old cog train engine is on display.

On the south edge of Manitou Springs are the summits of Red Mountain and Iron Mountain. They are convenient to town and a short hike will immediately place you

Distance: 4.5 miles

Difficulty: 🌲🌲🌲🌲🌲

Elevation Gain: 800 feet

into the forest and mountain air that we all crave. We often don't realize how much it was needed until we are in the pines, and this hike is just one of the many examples that we all have within a short distance of town.

For the overachieving readers, you may wish to combine this chapter with the Iron Mountain chapter to double the length of your hike.

Red Mountain Incline's lower station on Ruxton Avenue
Photo courtesy of Old Colorado Historical Society
Luther McKnight Collection

Getting There: Park in a free public parking lot in downtown Manitou Springs. From here, look uphill to the south and spot the two summits. Iron Mountain is on the left with the lone tree on top and Red Mountain is to the right. If you look carefully, you can spot the remnants of a concrete foundation hanging onto the left side of the summit that will be your destination today. Hop on the free shuttle that goes up Ruxton Avenue to the Incline. Half way up Ruxton Avenue you will spot the entrance to Miramont Castle. At this location, on your left, is where the base of the Red Mountain Incline was located. Nothing is left of this place now, but when you summit the top, you will be looking back down to this point to get a feel of where the tourists would have boarded the cable-hauled cars.

Get off the bus at the last bus stop **(1)** when the bus turns around. From the bus stop, walk downhill to immediately catch the Intemann Trail on your right. Check out the Iron Springs mineral spring **(2)** and then the classic stone bridge **(3)** just beyond. Turn right on Spring Street and then switchback right **(4)** on the dirt road. Cross over the heavy chain **(5)** that runs across the road.

The Hike: From the chain, you will briefly ascend up a steep dirt road. At the top of the road **(6)** is a gully with a concrete runoff control barrier. Your trail will bear left and then level out. Take a moment at the stone bench **(7)** to appreciate your first clear view of the picturesque little town in the valley below.

Just a bit farther along the trail you will encounter a very large level area **(8)**. It appears that this flat spot was manmade but long since overgrown and reclaimed by nature. Ready for a fun find? On your left as you enter the level clearing look down

21

into the little gulley. There is 1936 Ford Deluxe Touring Sedan lying on its roof **(9)** just a few feet below this trail. Not many hikers on this trail know of this hidden find. If they ask how you knew, promote this book!

A 1936 Ford Deluxe Touring Sedan in better shape

Soon after this clearing you will encounter the trail junction **(10)** to Red Mountain. Take the right fork uphill to the top of Red Mountain. (You will be returning back down this trail to continue the exploration of Intemann Trail to return to your vehicle.)

The 7/10 of a mile hike gains elevation quickly with a few switchbacks. The woods become dense. The trail winds in and out of shade. You have just been transported from an urban trail into the forest. In the cooler months, expect icy spots in the shadows.

As you near the top of your hike, the summit will appear as a granite outcropping above you and to the left. Emma Crawford began her celebrated descent very near to this spot.

At this saddle **(11)** just before the summit, you will spot a faint trail that runs uphill to the right. How can a trail run uphill from a summit, you ask? As you can imagine, there are many places called "Red Mountain" in the state of Colorado. From this point of view you can tell that Manitou Springs's Red Mountain isn't really a mountain summit at all, but more of a point on the end of a ridge jutting out from the much bigger mountain behind. It looks like a summit from town, and that's what counts.

The final piece of your ascent is to climb through the narrow notch in the granite **(12)** to find the floor of a dance hall on top. Surprise! Some roof support pillars can still easily be seen on the perimeter.

Imagine the wooden building that held the dance hall sitting on top of this rock and a smaller building that covered the hoist. There was a 12-foot high sign advertising the Red Mountain Incline in an attempt to attract the tourists. This ambitious attraction lasted for only 10 years from 1912 to 1922.

To your right are a set of concrete steps going down to the hoist house for the cable cars. Once the riders reached the top,

Red Mountain Dance Hall and hoist house
Photo courtesy of Old Colorado City Historical Society
Luther McKnight Collection

they would have ascended these steps to get to the main building. On the foundation of the hoist house are the heavy bolts that held the powerful cable hoist.

You have gained 800 feet of elevation. It is time to admire the 360-degree view that is your reward for the short steep hike to the top of Red Mountain, and what a view it is. If you look just below Pikes Peak you can see Engelmann Canyon. This canyon is the route of the Pikes Peak cog train. On the left edge above the canyon you can easily spot the prominent knob of Magog Rock. I had always thought that was a Native American name, but Tim tells me the name has early biblical origins going back to the Book of Genesis.

The vertical line to the right of Engelmann Canyon is the top of the Mount Manitou Incline. You can almost feel the ongoing "elevation celebrations" happening up there right now. You are viewing this from the summit of your own incline hike, but without the crowds and without the pain. Congratulations! You can now post that you made it to the top of the incline in Manitou and its okay to skip the specifics by conveniently omitting which incline.

To the right of the incline is Ute Pass, the Native American path that turned into a major supply corridor for the miners of the last century and now contains Highway 24. Near the top and to the left of Ute Pass is the Ferris wheel at Santa's North Pole. Continuing your view to the right, the switchback road on the other side of Highway 24 leading to Cave of the Winds is quite visible. Can you spot the Cliff Dwellings in the valley to the right of the Cave of the Winds? Panning to the right, the dramatic sight of Garden of the Gods dominates the view. Down below, Manitou Springs looks like an alpine village and the entirety of Colorado Springs may be seen from city limit to city limit.

Visually follow along Highway 24 that runs west above Manitou Springs and you can clearly see the tall bridge that stretches above Williams Canyon. This canyon is filled with mysterious caves and once was the exit road from Cave of the Winds, quite appropriately named The Narrows. There is also an excellent view of the highway's hillside cuts that expose the uplifted layers, created when the Rocky Mountains were formed. The angle of the layers is reflected in the landscape all along the front range.

To the east, you get a good view of the top of nearby Iron Mountain that is the next chapter in this book. Uphill behind you is Crystal Hills, a gated housing community with plenty of land and almost unlimited views. Are you envious of what their view must be like at sunrise or the city lights at night? So are we.

Take your time at the summit. Sit down and feel the breeze. Listen to the hum of the town below. Now see if you can spot the large Miramont Castle below and then find the short road that connects it to Ruxton Avenue. The lower terminus for the Red Mountain Incline was at this intersection. Imagine the straight line the incline would have followed. An overgrown cut through a mound below is all that can be seen of this route today. When this cable-hauled line was in operation, it ran through two cuts and over a wooden trestle. This location for the base station was chosen because it was very visible to the tourists going to the better known Manitou Incline, but more importantly, it runs over the top of the tunnel for the railroad, eliminating an awkward crossing of the tracks.

When you are ready, return back down the same trail you came up on, to rejoin **(10)** Intemann Trail. Turn right on Intemann Trail to continue the adventure. Very quickly you will encounter an overlook with a single tree **(13)**. This is a good spot to check out the buildings below. After that you will spot a rugged road **(14)** going steeply uphill to your right. There is nothing much to see up there but some old piping, but this is very near where the incline crossed the trail. Back on the trail, a junction **(15)** leads to the neighborhood below, but continue straight ahead. After the trail junction you encounter the odd sight of a metal road barrier **(16)** with remnants of yellow paint blocking a nonexistent roadway. Far from a road, this route shows up on the maps as a city street but hasn't been used except for utility access for a very, very long time. Soon after this, you will encounter a fork **(17)** in the trail. The lesser trail to the right leads to nothing in particular. Keep to the right.

When you hit the paved Pawnee Road **(18)** go left downhill to return to Manitou Avenue and your car. If you would choose to turn right going uphill on Pawnee Road you will find the continuation of Intemann Trail about 50 feet up that will lead to the summit of Iron Mountain **(19)** in the next chapter.

Cars passing on the trestle
Detail from an early Red Mountain Incline brochure

A Step Farther:
The slide into history

What *could* be found of Emma is buried in the Crystal Valley Cemetery, the principal graveyard in Manitou Springs. Bits of Emma have been discovered throughout the years and I presume those were added to her interment site.

The cemetery—established in 1882, listed in the National Register of Historic Places—is located on Plainview Place, and has a good view of Red Mountain. If you were to take a side trip to this historic cemetery, and walked the gravesite rows, you would come upon a headstone that reads: "In Memoriam, Emma L. Crawford, Passed to the Higher Life, December 4th 1891, She Will Not Be Forgotten." And, indeed she was not.

In the late 1800s, Emma came to Manitou Springs with her mother. Emma was very sick with tuberculosis, and had traveled to Colorado seeking the healing qualities of the mineral water in this area of the state. It seemed that between the cool, dry air at this elevation, and the mineral-infused, natural effervescent water, she was able to beat her ailment. She became engaged, but, unfortunately, encountered another bout of her illness and died a few days prior to her wedding. She had just trail hiked up Red Mountain. This had been a goal for her, and upon her summit, she tired a red scarf around a tree.

After Emma's passing, her fiancé William Hildebrand (a civil engineer on the Pikes Peak Cog Railway) and 11 other men carried her coffin near to the top of Red Mountain to bury her, despite not having the proper permits, fulfilling a death bed wish of Emma's. Some years later, after days of heavy rain, the soaked soil gave way to a landslide that brought her tumbling casket back into town. Over the years, various bones of poor Emma have been found, including her skull.

Is this the stuff of legend or fact? Either way, this story is part of the rich history of the Pikes Peak Region. And Emma was not forgotten.

Since 1995, Manitou Springs has held an event to honor Emma. The annual Emma Crawford Coffin Races and Parade (just before Halloween) commemorates her role in the town's history. Thousands of festival spectators line downtown's Manitou Avenue to cheer 50 coffin racing teams from all over the country. The race is preceded by a parade of caskets and antique hearses. (http://www.emmacrawfordfestival.com)

Racing teams consist of four running pallbearers and one "Emma," inside the coffin on wheels. Two teams at a time race uphill towards the finish line 195 yards away

A gruesome slide down a mountainside became the origin of one of the Pikes Peak Region's quirkiest traditions. Emma may have wanted to have been remembered for something else in her life (or death), yet here she is, honored for her last ride down Red Mountain.

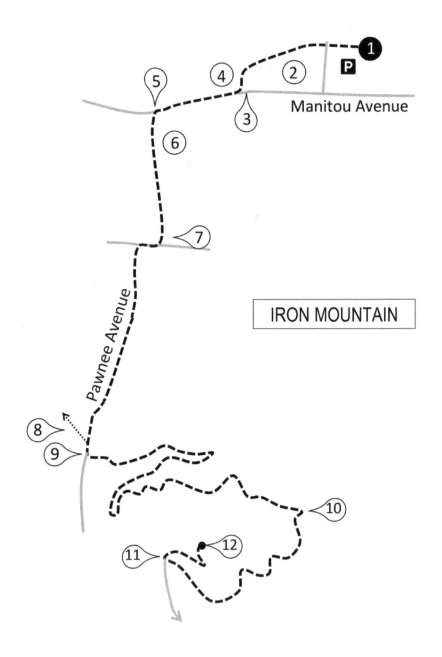

Manitou Avenue

IRON MOUNTAIN

Pawnee Avenue

3
Iron Mountain

The comeback story of
the little peak on the left

Iron Mountain sits above Manitou Springs and can easily be recognized from town as the smaller summit on the left. Close to town with easy access, this hike is not as treed as the adjacent Red Mountain but is a good hike in its own right.

Like all of the trails in this book, this little mountain has a story, but Iron Mountain's story does not start out as a cheerful tale. Take heart, though, there is a happy ending. This is a story of a potential developer that was upset when the town rejected a proposal to build 30 very visible homes on 100 acres above town on Iron Mountain and the adjacent Sheep Mountain. This denial was understandable as Iron Mountain is a prominent part of the backdrop to Manitou Springs and having a development so visible would have permanently damaged the view above town.

To spite the town's leaders for this rejection, an eyesore of a house was built on the summit of Iron Mountain. A road was attempted across the face of the mountain but the city was successful in blocking that potential scar. The home was a two story white rectangle that stood out in the backdrop of the beautiful town.

At that same time, the Intemann trail was being constructed along the edge of town to connect Manitou Springs to Colorado

Springs' trail system. Only one piece was missing, and you guessed it, the only gap for many years was created by the refusal of access by the same landowner along the edge of this property on Iron Mountain. That is more than enough negativity, now on to the good news.

In 2013, after two decades of hard feelings and disputes, the town was able to purchase the property and demolish the house while the population cheered in the little town below. The Intemann Trail was connected and is now open for exploration. As a bonus, a public trail was also built to the summit for our promised happy ending.

This adventure will take you along part of the Intemann Trail to the summit of Iron Mountain for a quick 800 foot elevation gain. You will then return by the same route.

This summit will have the hills close behind you so it's a good idea to keep your eyes open for clouds appearing quickly. In any hike, even more so when you have a higher ridge to your west, it is good advice to watch for heavy clouds surprising you above the close horizon. Even on a blue sky day, when the clouds show up, they can appear quickly and give little notice before nature reminds us who is really in control.

Getting There: The closest parking can be found in the free Hiawatha Gardens public parking lot **(1)** next to Manitou's Memorial Park. Walk west through the park **(2)** past a cannon and on to the antique steam engine **(3)** on display nearby. On the other side of the stone bridge sits Manitou Springs City Hall, police station, an air raid siren and most importantly, public restrooms **(4)** on the side of the building.

Follow Manitou Avenue one block west then cross the street **(5)** to walk up Pawnee Avenue. Yes, it's a steep city street, but you will be at the trailhead in one half mile.

Of course you want to ask why walk up the steep Pawnee Avenue when you can easily drive up to the trailhead. Parking is almost non-existent and what are found are mostly awkward spots in front of local resident's homes. Our reason though is that you get to pass by some great old houses, fences and gardens with eclectic décor and this is about the total exploration, not cutting it short. As soon as you start up Pawnee Avenue on your left **(6)** is the oldest congregational church in Colorado. Across the street is the Manitou Springs Carnegie Library.

The Hike: As you ascend Pawnee Avenue, your route jogs to the right on Midland Avenue **(7)** for a very short distance then continues uphill on Pawnee Avenue. Follow this road with the concrete culvert running down the middle. Just before the road narrows you can see Iron Mountain looming above you directly ahead. The summit doesn't look that far away, does it? Note your trail cutting horizontally across the middle of the mountain. Look up and to the right for a good view of the concrete foundation on top of Red Mountain. You will pass a sign that states Residents Only, but you are permitted to continue to the trailhead. Before you know it, the Intemann trailhead **(8)** will appear on your right. This takes you to Red Mountain as experienced in the previous chapter. Pass it by and

33

continue uphill on the road for another 50 yards to the trailhead on your left **(9)** for your start up Iron Mountain.

From the Pawnee Avenue trailhead follow the Intemann trail east as it switchbacks up the face of Iron Mountain. At the first switchback the panorama immediately opens up as the Garden of the Gods formations pop into view giving you an idea of the treats to follow.

Iron Mountain (7,136 feet) and Red Mountain (7,375 feet)

As the trail wraps around the mountain **(10)**, the view changes to the expanse of the plains to the east. On the face of hillside across the valley to your right, is the continuation of the Ring the Peak trail and the Intemann Trail. This trail takes you to the Red Rock Canyon Open Space and beyond. Look closely at the point where the trail disappears around the bend on the east end. At this large bare flat spot next to the trail is a medicine wheel.

Directly above the medicine wheel point are the tall buildings of Colorado Springs. Above the downtown city center is the dome over the Velodrome near Prospect Lake. From this vantage point, our city does not appear to be as big as we think it is. As you continue the hike, just around the corner, boom, large mountain homes suddenly appear.

Almost to the top you will intersect **(11)** a trail junction. Left goes to the medicine wheel and continues on to Red Rock

Canyon Open Space. On this hike, though, go right to quickly attain the summit **(12)**. Look for remnants of the home that used to be up here. There are signs but not much is to be found. Sit upon the summit and take a break. Have a snack and remember to hydrate. Absorb the views.

Can you spot the foundation of the hoist house clinging to the side of Red Mountain nearby? On the distant hillside to the west is a large water tank above town. Above and to the left of that tank is a taller water tank and building situated on the Ute Pass Trail.

Across the valley to the north is the serpentine road leading to the Cave of the Winds. On the horizon above the Cave of the Winds you can easily see the altered landscape of the destructive 2012 Waldo Canyon Fire. Note how well you can see the Cliff Dwellings from this elevation. See if you can spot the curved SunWater Spa building below and your parking lot nearby. Below and to the right is the primo location of the Manitou Springs High School. Lucky kids.

If you wish, take the trail one half mile more to the medicine wheel and beyond to Red Rock Canyon Open Space by going straight ahead as you descend the summit.

If you decide to take this side trip to this wheel after you summit Iron Mountain, it will only add one mile round trip to your hike. Before you get to the site, you may want to find the perfect rock and bring it with you for your contribution. That public wheel near Iron Mountain has grown considerably and it just feels right to add your piece to this endeavor.

If you are returning the way you came, go left, and then you now know the way from here!

A Step Farther:
The penny arcade and the boulder

Want to experience a historical *treasure* ... for just pennies? Take a walk down memory lane just off the main drag in Manitou Springs by visiting the historic Penny Arcade. This visit is really fun for all ages.

About four blocks west of the end of your Iron Mountain hike in the historic center of town, you can become a kid again by finding hundreds of working, vintage arcade games, including pinball, Skee Ball and racing games—some 100 years old. The arcades are actually located in several little buildings, each with its own style and feel. Some store fronts feel like you are in a place that hasn't changed much since the early 1900s. Be sure to observe the photos above the games for a pictorial history of the arcade from the early days.

In the arcade buildings, be sure to find the 12-person mechanical horseracing track. If that isn't enough, the little ones can enjoy coin-operated kiddie rides from the Batmobile to a pink elephant in a pavilion in the center of the arcade. But wait, there's more! Go back in time to view images from the past on Mutoscopes—early motion picture devices for just one person, developed in 1894. Bring a pocket full of coins from pennies to quarters. The arcade is only open if the weather is 50 degrees or warmer.

On the back wall of Patsy's Candies in the arcade is the Navajo Spring. This least visible mineral spring in town is still running. The font is attached to the back of the building that was once the tasting room for the mineral water bottling company. Just past the arcade on the next street, you can also enjoy a visit to the Cliff House for more historical photos of the area.

The covered walkway between the buildings of the Royal Tavern and the Cliff House used to be called Pike Street. Bits of the curbs and sidewalks can still be seen. The gentleman that owned the greenstone quarry in Manitou Springs closed Pike Street in 1930 to create a walking mall and installed the greenstone columns to support a roof over what was once a city street.

A superstar of this area's history is all but hidden underground. Between the Penny Arcade and the Manitou Spa building is the large round top of an exposed boulder. For fun, climb on top and envision the size of this round rock. The bottom of the boulder is resting on the original stream bed. If you look at the creek under the bridge, it is running at the original elevation of the valley. Over the decades of development, the surrounding area has been filled in, leaving the boulder in place with only the top showing.

Then and now; the first photo shows this boulder next to the stream in 1881. The second photo was taken from about the same angle today. What once was a landmark is still appreciated as a mountain for the little ones to climb up next to the rides.

This is a beneficial stop for several reasons. After the Iron Mountain hike, play some Skee Ball, run a horse race, climb on a rock, explore the Spa Building as well as the hallways of the Cliff House. And remember to take home some Patsy's world-famous caramel corn.

Manitou Arcade boulder in 1881 and today
1881 detail from a stereograph, courtesy of
Special Collections, Pikes Peak Library District   175-3683

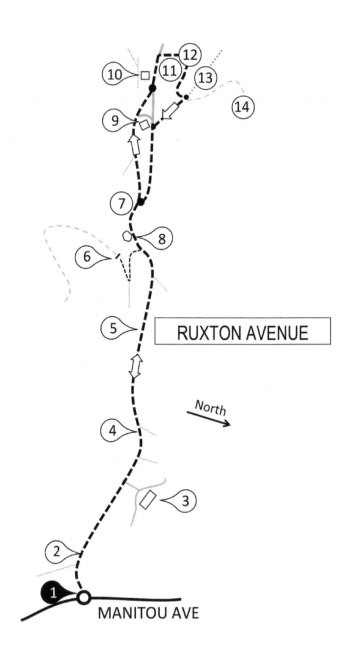

RUXTON AVENUE

North

MANITOU AVE

40

4
Ruxton Avenue

Uphill on a short road through time

The unique mountain town of Manitou Springs has a wealth of interesting locations to explore. There are two streamside city parks and an antique penny arcade with operating relics that seek modern coins. There is the old mineral spring bath house with shops, lofts, restaurants, its own mineral spring and creekside dining. There are scores of shops and restaurants in fantastic old buildings. The Pikes Peak and Manitou Cog Railway, Cave of the Winds, the Barr Trail, Mount Manitou Incline, zip lines and The Manitou Cliff Dwellings are all well worth visiting, but this book is about what is beyond!

On this walk, we're going to explore some items that the typical tourist may drive right by. This slice of Manitou is a good walk with history along the way and plenty to experience. You can see most of these points from your car, but doesn't it feel good to get out and walk in this fresh Colorado air? Parking is always a premium in Manitou Springs and we suggest using one of the downtown parking lots and then strolling through town to the roundabout at Ruxton Avenue and Manitou Avenue.

Although it is hard to imagine today, nineteenth century explorers could have traveled from New York City directly to the summit of Pikes Peak solely by rail without having to do more than change rail cars. The traveler would transfer from one train onto another without the inconvenience of soiling their city attire, avoiding equine-powered transportation altogether. It was the simple matter of taking the railroad from Denver to Colorado Springs and then hopping on the trolley that ran through Colorado City and Manitou Springs, terminating at the end of Ruxton Avenue. At that point the traveler would board the steam powered cog train to the summit of Pikes Peak.

Distance: 2 miles

Difficulty:

Elevation Gain: 350 ft

There were two railroads that ran to downtown Manitou Springs, and we'll see some remnants of those on this walk. The Midland Railroad ran from the historic roundhouse seen at the intersection of Highway 24 and 21st Street (now a restaurant and retail shops). The Denver and Rio Grande Western, (D&RGW) ran south from Denver but had a spur into Manitou Springs. A relative that worked in the mines of Colorado said that the miners joked that the D&RGW initials stood for Dangerous and Rapidly Growing Worse.

Ruxton Avenue is less than a mile long and you will be returning back down this same road. Start your exploration from the roundabout. The world famous Chicago Loop was named for the interurban trolley's lakeside turn around. That's where the similarity ends. The Manitou Loop at the intersection of Manitou Avenue and Ruxton Avenue **(1)** was the trolley turnaround on a circular track. At this intersection, the long standing Loop Restaurant's name celebrates this location. There was also a spur of the trolley line, nicknamed the Dinky Trolley that went from this tight circle of track uphill along Ruxton Avenue and terminated at the Pikes Peak Cog train depot.

On the roundabout is a sculpture of a young girl dispensing the mineral laden waters of Stratton Spring. This is the first of three mineral springs that you will be passing on your exploration uphill. As each spring has a different mineral content, it is advised to bring along a cup for tastings. Several more mineral springs are found throughout Manitou that flow cool and refreshing year round. Locals will bring gallon jugs to fill and take home, adding fruit juice for a flavorful effervescent drink.

The restaurant currently inhabited by The Loop Mexican Restaurant was built in 1903 and specialized in local wild game such as bear, mountain lion and elk. The fireplace and piano bar in the main level are quite old and gambling was said to be upstairs. Behind the building are the brick fire pits that have not been used for decades and can be glimpsed in the alley.

The Hike: Remaining on the left side of the street, begin the uphill walk. At 121 Ruxton Avenue you will find the second natural mineral spring on this walk. Twin Springs mineral spring **(2)** is actually mounted on the front of the building. Twin Springs is arguably the best tasting spring in Manitou Springs. I also propose that Wheeler Spring downtown near the Cliff House is the worst tasting spring. What is your opinion?

As you continue walking uphill you can't help but notice the different types of stairways built on either side of the canyon to reach a nice array of homes from the early 1900s. Curio shops along the right side of the street are evidence that this has been a tourist destination since the area was first promoted in east coast publications. Many of the multiple small square block buildings with glass fronts are now converted to residences but several still hold eclectic goods for your exploration.

At the intersection with Capitol Hill Avenue (3) you can see the historic Miramont Castle. Guided tours of the castle and museum, teas and light meals can make for a leisurely stop. Across the street and just a bit uphill was the bottom terminal (4) for the Red Mountain Incline. No remnants are left of the lower station, but you can hike to the top in another chapter.

Continuing uphill just before the creek crosses under the road (5) at 355 Ruxton Avenue, you will see a dirt cutoff on

Trolley tracks to the left and Ruxton Ave to the right

your left, now used for residential parking. The trolley rails are still visible! At this point the trolley left the middle of the road and ran up the left side of the creek. Stay on Ruxton Avenue as it continues along the right side of Ruxton Creek.

At Spring Street, on your left, walk one block up to the start of Intemann Trail. This trail is popular with the locals and will lead you to Red Rock Open Space and on to the Gold Camp Road. You will see markers for the Ring the Peak Trail, an ambitious undertaking that encircles Pikes Peak. Just after the chain **(6)** marking the start of the trail, immediately to your left, is a train tunnel cut into the granite. Still intact and well hidden by weeds and time, many townsfolk have forgotten it is there. It is surprisingly close to the road but well hidden from the casual explorer. Marked by no trespassing signs, you can spot the dark entrance in the hillside above the trail. After exiting the tunnel, the railroad immediately crossed a very high trestle over this canyon and Ruxton Avenue.

There are a series of abandoned railroad tunnels from this route that parallel Highway 24 west of town. They are easily spotted while driving up Ute Pass, but unfortunately they are almost inaccessible for exploration.

Now return back down to Ruxton Avenue. Just before Ruxton, turn left on the Intemann Trail and look for an iron beam in the bushes on your left and a concrete block in the creek that are remnants of the trestle that crossed Ruxton Avenue high overhead.

Across the street it is possible to see the roadbed where the bridge connected. A notable train wreck occurred on this trestle in 1909 when several freight cars fell onto Ruxton Avenue. See if you can spot the boulder **(8)** that is still next to the road, shown on the right of this photo.

Iron Spring **(7)** is your third and final mineral spring on this walk. A modern sculpture adorns the font under the gazebo.

Immediately up Ruxton Avenue you will encounter the Iron Springs Chateau. The small dirt road running towards the cog station from the Iron Springs Chateau's parking lot **(9)** is the last bit of the trolley's roadbed.

Use caution crossing the unusual traffic alignment and continue up to the depot for the Pikes Peak and Manitou Cog Railway **(10)**. Take a break at the snack bar, check out the old photographs and share the excitement of the passengers leaving and returning from the summit of Pikes Peak.

Top: Remnants of the bridge
Bottom: Ruxton Avenue train wreck 1909
Lower Photograph by Margaretta Boas Courtesy of
Special Collections, Pikes Peak Library District   001-8334

When you are ready, continue on up the hill one more block. Spend a moment to look over the railing at the cog train's facilities. Turn right after the old brick hydroelectric power plant **(11)** on the right side of the road. This plant is well over 100 years old and is still producing electricity.

The last part of your uphill trek on Hydro Street is also the steepest part of your hike but don't despair, as it's only about a half block long. Really steep! You have reached the base of Barr Trail **(12)**. This 13-mile trail (one way) ascends to the 14,115 foot summit of Pikes Peak. You will be pleased to know that you are now at the high point of your hike. Locate a dirt trail on the right side of the tiny parking lot that will circle behind the power station and descend to the start of the Manitou Incline **(13)**.

Pause to look up and imagine what it feels like to take those 2,744 stairs to the top. To the right of the incline **(14)** is the beginning of the unpaved Ute Pass Trail. Provide encouragement to the intrepid hikers on the start of their climb as you blissfully know that you are going downhill from here.

Hopefully you will return to take the cog train to the summit. You may return to dine and boo the villain at the historic Iron Spring Chateau's melodrama theater. Maybe you will return to do all or part of the Barr Trail, attempt the Manitou Incline, explore the Ute Pass Trail, or even the Ring the Peak Trail. This little dead end road ties to an abundance of fun times.

Who was Ruxton and why did he get a road named after him? Thanks for asking. George F. Ruxton was an Englishman, an author and a wild-west adventurer. He fell in love with the beauties of Ute Pass and praised it in his 1840s book, *Life in the Far West*, well before the towns of Manitou Springs and

Colorado Springs existed. Thirty years later, Ruxton Creek was given its name by George Cameron, a business partner with General William Palmer, the founder of Colorado Springs and the D&RGW. Ruxton Avenue followed later. George Cameron named Cameron's Cone after himself, the most prominent formation above this valley.

Your walk up Ruxton is now rewarded by the downhill counterpart. Near the end of your hike notice how Ruxton Creek actually runs underneath some of the buildings and admire the stonework of the bridges. After your exploration, it is nice to know that an icy beverage is waiting for you in town.

A Step Farther:
Stairways and doorways

I've always been fascinated by historic stairs. I've enjoyed discovering them, determining their purpose, and photographing them. Coming from Southern California, I'd visit old concrete stairs at tidal shores, worn down by time and crashing waves, leading to long-passed oceanfront property, the foundation work now a saltwater pool.

Now that I live in Colorado, I visit stone stairs on trails that lead into and out of lush forests and up to the top of mountains, and those that ascend to historic sites of yesteryear. The vintage railroad tie stairs up the Manitou Incline climb to exhilaration and thin air celebration upon completion, as well as to explorations of remnants from bygone days.

That's one thing about stairs: they take you somewhere, or they did at one time. Stairs are directional and lead you to a destination. Sometimes you can see where they are taking you, and other times the adventure is in not knowing where you are going. Yet we start, one step at a time.

The exploration on Ruxton Avenue takes you past many historic stairs, most to lovely old homes, some stairs stone, some wood, many lined with overflowing pots or beds of summer flowers. Most of the stairs are worn from the many years of pat-pat-pat footsteps up and down. Many climb right up to the front of the homes on either side of the tree lined walk.

Stairs may take you to doors. Doors open to homes, and inside, homes are filled with so many memories. As I walked up Ruxton, I couldn't help think about how many stories were carried up and down the stairs, and in and out of these front doors through the years.

Ruxton Avenue is filled with rich history, and the stops along the way pay evidence to that. Countless tales of individuals and families are only imagined as you pause at each set of stairs and doorways along this narrow street. I wonder what new stories are being created today?

Unlike the other maps, this map is not to scale. It represents the area above the incline but does not include the hike up Barr Trail or the Incline.
We suggest this exploration only if you are going to be up there anyway.
The exploration is not difficult but getting there is. Know your capabilities.

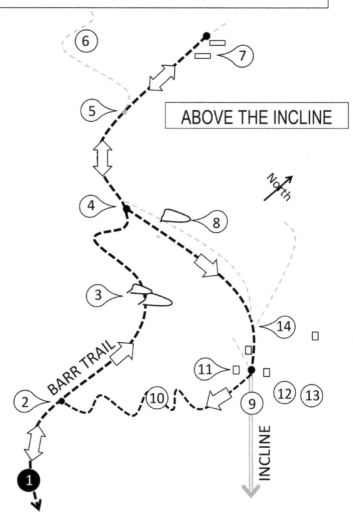

ABOVE THE INCLINE

5

Above the Incline

*What lies beyond where
everybody else turns around?*

Above the quaint town of Manitou Springs, just west of
Colorado Springs, is a vertical scar running up the side of the
mountain. Easy to spot and well known locally, the Mount
Manitou Incline was initially built as a temporary method to
haul pipeline up the steep mountainside above the picturesque
town and later was adapted as a popular tourist attraction.

Utilizing two rail cars connected by a single cable and
powered by a large mine hoist at the top of the hill, those two
counterbalanced cars would pass each other half way up the
track. This style of transportation is known as a funicular
railway and the term applies to a functional working incline as
well as it does to a tourist's ride with a breathtaking view. Our
word of the day is funicular.

The rails were in use from 1904 until 1989 when the
attraction was closed and the rails were removed, leaving the
ties as a natural stairway. Quickly discovered by intrepid, and
trespassing, hikers and fitness buffs, these steep stairs became
quite popular. This mile long route gains over 2,000 feet in
elevation and became a legitimate public trail in 2014. The

Mount Manitou Incline is one of the busiest trails in the state, but there are numerous interesting areas just above this climb that most people don't visit and that is what interests us the most!

Did you know that a peak called Rocky Mountain Peak is one of the Rocky Mountains? You would think it would be one of the 14,000 foot peaks in Colorado, but Rocky Mountain Peak is the official name of the

Distance: 3 miles on top
Not counting the hike to get there

Difficulty: 🌲🌲🌲🌲🌲 !

Elevation Gain: 2,800 feet

mountain that you will be climbing. Mount Manitou is actually behind this one. Feel free to brag to your friends about conquering Rocky Mountain without providing too many specifics.

Getting started: Arriving at the area above the Incline may not be an extreme hike to some, but this is the most difficult exploration in this book. This adventure isn't about the Incline, but what can be found above it. Don't worry; you don't have to do the Incline itself to reach the exploration of the artifacts beyond. OK, worry, because the alternative is several miles of the Barr Trail. We suggest this exploration if you are going to be up there anyway.

The alternative route to the top of the Incline is the lower portion of the Barr Trail. Barr Trail is less taxing but a longer hike that will take you to the exact same destination. Beyond the scope of this chapter, the well maintained trail of switchbacks will ultimately zig-zag 13 miles up the eastern face of Pikes Peak to reach the summit, but you will be happy to know that we're only interested in the first three miles for this hike. We suggest using Barr Trail because this book is about the exploration and you will have more energy for the adventure at the top. We prefer this route when we explore the extensive trails above the Incline and will still be able to hop over and join in the "Elevation Celebration" of those arriving at the top via the Manitou Incline.

Don't try to park at the top of Ruxton Avenue, take the free shuttle in town. At the end of Ruxton Avenue, after you pass behind the Iron Springs Chateau and before you approach the cog train station, bear right up a very short and steep drive leading to a parking lot above and to your right.

Let's check out the base of the Incline first. See if you can spot the old passenger loading area in the parking lot below, directly in line with the Incline. It is filled in now, but the loading area is still there, as well as the bases of the iron I beams that held up the roof. The car would end in a pit that allowed the passenger to step directly into the seating area. The iron edge of the loading pit is still clearly visible. Inside the building next to this loading platform the ticket window is still visible inside the gift shop.

As you look uphill at the first of the 2,700 railroad wooden tie steps that make up the Incline, you can imagine the challenge! To the right of the start of the Incline is the beginning of the Ute Pass Trail, found in another chapter of this book.

Here's a thought to ponder while you walk up Barr Trail: On the Incline, why did the track have three rails at the top, four rails in the middle and two rails at the bottom? See the graphic.

Answer: Since there were two cars joined by a single cable, the top half had to be wide enough to pass. Only three rails were needed on the top half because the center rail could be shared, causing the cable from the other car to be dangerously close enough to touch. The four rails in the middle section were where the cars passed. Only two rails were needed below the passing point as there would never be more than one car at a time on these tracks and no cable to avoid.

Once an incline hiker makes it to the top, the encouragement and congratulations from the others that they have encountered add to the exhilaration of completing the climb. During one of my early Incline hikes, a group of Fort Carson army personnel in civilian attire were using the Incline for an early morning workout. Cheering and chiding each other, they made it to the top well before I did. At more than twice their age, I stopped on a very steep section near the top for a drink of water and heard the group shouting from above, "Don't stop, keep moving!" I was quite energized when I realized that they were talking to me! As I looked back down from this steep area they shouted almost in unison, "Don't look down!" When I looked up to give them an appreciative smile, one shouted, "Don't look up either!" Needless to say, there were a lot of high fives at the top. Once you reach the top of any ascent, take a break, take a selfie, hydrate, enjoy the views and congratulate the hikers arriving behind you. You have all earned it!

The Hike: From this parking lot at the base of the Incline, walk to the left of the Incline to find a dirt trail that will lead to the base of the Barr Trail. Climbing gradually along the first three miles of Barr Trail to our destination should take you about two hours at a moderate pace. These lower switchbacks **(1)** are busy with the incliners coming back down. For the first 20 minutes of your hike you can see and hear the cog train in the valley below. At approximately 1.75 miles into the hike you will encounter an overlook to the Incline where you may watch the intrepid Incline hikers about two-thirds the way through their own vertical workout. This is a point that the hard working incliners may pull out and access the Barr Trail. (There is also a return path on the north side of the incline that drops onto the Ute Pass Trail, another chapter in this book.)

Near the two mile mark, you will see a set of landscape timber stairs **(2)** that the Incline hikers will use to spill out from the top of the Incline onto Barr Trail for their return back down to the start. Continue straight up the trail for now as you will be circling around and coming back down these stairs after your explorations. From this point on, without the incliners, the trail will be much less crowded. Near the 2.5 mile mark you will get your first view of Pikes Peak. The summit looks a lot closer now! Soon after this view you will pass through a natural keyhole under huge boulders **(3)** for a fun photo opportunity.

Not long after passing under these boulders you will reach an intersection **(4)** with the first of several very old iron signs. The distances are not correct, but close enough for the pre-GPS era. This is where the "exploration beyond the attraction" really begins. Above you to the right the sign directs you to the route back to the top of the Incline, but don't take that path just yet. When you come back down you will taking this short trail to the top of the Incline and then down those wooden steps back to the Barr Trail. For now, continue straight on up Barr Trail. Yes, more uphill. Don't hate. We warned you this trail was challenging, but the effort is worth it!

It is only a short distance to another split in the trail **(5)** and a second old iron sign. To the left of the sign is a great old log that has provided decades of hikers a welcome rest. Near here, the stream has a small waterfall trickling underneath a huge boulder. Take a break and enjoy the serenity.

The sign gives the option go left nine more miles **(6)** to the summit of Pikes Peak or to the right for a quarter mile to the Fremont Experimental Forest. Easy choice; go right.

In the early 20th century The Fremont Experimental Forest **(7)** was an attempt to determine what types of trees could exist

Building and stairs: Fremont Experimental Forest

at this elevation and location. In hindsight, we can imagine that no one was too surprised when they discovered that only the native trees remained. Quite a few foundations, walkways and stairs have endured for your exploration.

It has been said that some of the mature pine trees can still be seen planted in neat rows but we haven't been able to find them. Maybe you can! These historical foundations are at the highest elevation of your exploration.

The rough dirt road continues on to Ute Pass and a junction with the Ute Trail that leads back to Manitou Springs, but that is a much bigger adventure for another day. This road is protected by a locked gate off of Highway 24. Now return back the way you came, past the junction to the Pikes Peak summit and on down to the first iron sign you encountered on the way up. Take the left fork up **(4)** to the top of the Incline. This is a rustic Forest Service road. As an option, there is a trail that parallels to the left of this road that will take you under another granite boulder underpass, this one **(8)** with a very low clearance. Both the trail and the road will lead you to the same place.

A low clearance on the side trail

At the top of the Mount Manitou Incline, **(9)** take time to appreciate the sweeping view of the city below. Marvel at your 2,000-ft elevation gain. You may also be glad that you didn't have to arrive by those stairs! From here you can spot the Garden of the Gods Park, Cave of the Winds, the parking lot at the base of the Incline, the city of Manitou Springs and Colorado Springs, and beyond. What a view!

On the ride up this funicular, the guide manning the cable that pulled the cars would explain the safety measures built into the system as it was pretty obvious that traditional brakes would not work on such a steep track. The guide would state that if all else failed there are two large springs at the bottom to stop your rapid descent. Manitou Springs and Colorado Springs, a joke repeated on the cog train today.

Left: A lone water tank taken from a cog railway engine

Congratulate those exhausted but exhilarated incliners that reach the top. When you are ready, turn around and face uphill with your back to the Incline. Now it's time to find the artifacts and remnants of what was at one time a very busy tourist destination. Directly ahead of you is the bulky U shaped foundation of the hoist house that powered the single cable for the two cars. You can still see the mounting for the machinery. Just above the hoist is a square pad of concrete with a circular pattern and four protruding bolts. This was for the coin operated binoculars that you find at many tourist attractions. To your extreme left is the shortcut down to Barr Trail **(10)** and your eventual route back down. Next to this trailhead down is the foundation and steps **(11)** of the original caretaker's home.

To the immediate right of the top of the Incline are the minimal remains of the snack bar **(12)** and gift shop. Follow the trail behind this foundation, to your north, past the "T" shaped concrete wall and foundation which were the old restrooms. Near the restroom foundation is an old water tank **(13)** from the side of an 1890s Pikes Peak Cog Train steam engine. Far from the cog train's tracks, they must have hauled it up the Incline for water storage.

Beyond this tank are unique picnic tables built from iron train rails. These overly sturdy picnic tables from another era should be around for centuries. The salvaged rails are dated 1887. Next to the four ancient picnic tables is an overgrown set of steps.

(14) You may spot a sign for a trail that is almost gone. Called the Eagles Nest, this was a lighted hiking trail up until the 1960s. Those lights on the Eagles Nest trail in addition to the lights that lit the Incline's vertical ascent created the shape of a mountain-sized question mark of lights that could  be seen for miles. If you wish to explore this short but steep trail to Eagles Nest, note that the upper half of the trail has disappeared over the years. To get to the top of the overlook, visualize the question mark shape and circle around it to the right. Since there is no visible trail in this area, be quite cautious about selecting your course coming back down so as not to miss your route back to the top of the Incline.

Now that you are ready to go down, don't be tempted to take the Incline down; prohibited for safety reasons. From the top of the Incline, take the shortcut that you saw earlier to the left of the Incline (on your right now) to return to the Barr Trail and back down in about half the time it took you to climb up.

At the top of the incline, snack bar in the background.
Note the tilt of the camera to make it look even steeper.
Rocky is standing in the third row.

A Step Farther:
A treasure hunt

The sun shone brightly this morning, a welcome change after so many days of summer rain. Wispy clouds floated on a gentle breeze over the valley below. I chose to hike the Barr Trail for this beyond-the-attraction exploration. I had hiked this long trail, years earlier, doing the full 13 miles to the summit of Pikes Peak. I slowly huffed and puffed up what really is a very moderate, well-maintained hiking trail to the top of the Manitou Incline. I paced myself with short rest stops as this was still a 2,000-ft elevation gain to my destination.

Many of the explorations we offer in this book will take you to isolated, serene, get-away-from-the-crowds experiences. This is not one of those. There is a literal parade of hikers up and down the Barr Trail, at least until you reach the top of the Incline. But if you enjoy people-watching, listening in (briefly, in passing) to others' exchanges, and like chatting with fellow hikers about your shared experience, then this adventure is still for you.

Rocky had provided me with a list of relics to look for on this above-the-incline adventure, and a diagram to follow—a historical artifact treasure map, if you will. Some things were very evident; others were hard to find and took some Indiana Jones-style searching to make the discoveries. My exploration did feel like a treasure hunt, but for treasured recollections of times mostly forgotten, of items and buildings constructed for a purpose, their usefulness long passed, and of lives lived in and around these ghost objects from the past. Unlike a treasure hunt for riches however, I took away wonderful memories, golden moments reflecting on what life must have looked like on top of Mount Manitou back in the day.

I imagined the men and women in the early 1900s riding the Incline train to the top, with a similar breeze as today blowing across the open rail cars. All of the women are in dresses; all the men in suits and ties. All have hats on and they look like they are going to some evening social event, not a wilderness adventure.

In my mind's eye, I saw visitors disembark, stretch their legs, adjust their hats, and look down on jaw-dropping views of Manitou Springs, on to Colorado Springs and the prairie lands to the east beyond, just as the incline stair climbers do today, upon arriving at the summit. A few of the historic train riders still wore a grimaced look on their faces from what must have been a harrowing trip up the steep mountainside.

Some of the guests from bygone days now make their way to the snack bar and gift shop. A number had brought their own wicker baskets and wander over to the picnic tables made from iron train rails. Others hike up to Eagles Nest to take in the views of Ute Pass to the north. A few of the heartier walk farther to get an extraordinary view of Pikes Peak through the pines.

As I continued my hunt for remnant objects from the past (I even found some artifacts not on Rocky's list!) I came upon a hiker returning down from the Barr Trail back to the top of the Incline. He must have seen my notepapers, pen and the explorer's determination in the search.

"Find anything interesting up here?" he inquired. "Any hidden treasures?"

I smiled. "Well, as a matter of fact…"

Barr Trail

THE MOUNTAINS
TO THE WEST

Man's history is scattered throughout the mountains of the Pikes Peak region and there are countless trails to explore. We attempted to select a variety of treks that would offer the right combination of history and hike, but there is so much more for you to discover.

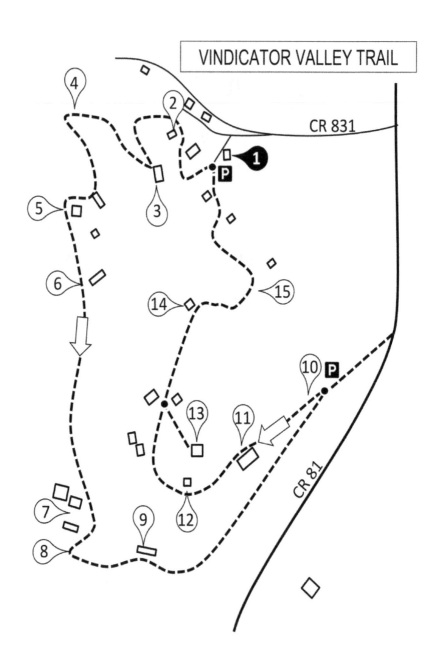

VINDICATOR VALLEY TRAIL

CR 831

CR 81

68

6

Vindicator Valley Trail

History not hidden

Just how much mining history can you cram into a two-mile loop? This hike passes some of the most famous mines in the Cripple Creek area as well as a gold mill, numerous lesser mines, the remnants of a power plant, and countless relics. Signage on this well-groomed trail illustrates the history, but as you would expect from this book, it's not just a hike. We will let the signs tell their stories while we find bits and pieces of hidden history along the way.

The backdrop of this hike is an imposing hillside created by a freshly relocated mountain. The Cripple Creek and Victor Mining Company has a very active open pit mine that is gradually overtaking the region. After your hike today, visit their overlook for this active mine to witness the gigantic trucks in action. If you can, we highly recommend that you take a tour provided by this company by making reservations through the Lowell Thomas Museum in Victor.

Don't mourn the loss of the natural landscape on this hike because this entire area was cleared and recreated in the way that best suited the gold miners 130 years ago. Note the absence of mature trees. Old photographs show this area was as barren as the moon ... well, if the moon had mines.

In the 1940s and again in the 1980s the landscape was once again rearranged. As the technology improved the ability to extract gold from the rocks, the mountains of tailings left by the previous generation were hauled off to be reprocessed. This is not a hike of natural beauty. This is a hike with an overabundance of artifacts.

Getting There: The town of Victor is five miles south of Cripple Creek on Highway 67. Victor is worth exploring for its buildings, shops, museum and mining equipment. After you explore downtown Victor follow Diamond Avenue above town and turn right. You will immediately encounter a junction that says to turn left for Highway 24 and right for Highway 50. This sign omits the fact that both highway options include miles of dirt roads to get to those highways. Bear to the left on County Road 81.

At this intersection on the edge of town is a large dirt parking lot with some mining equipment and informational signage. From this lot you can cross the street to explore the expansive remains of the Independence Mill. Once you have figured out what all of those concrete structures were for  (good luck!) continue on up CR 81 for 1.5 miles. After one mile you will see a trailhead **(10)** on the left with the very large Theresa Mine **(11)** nearby. Pass on by. We will be walking by this structure soon on our loop. Our entrance is just ahead.

Watch for two ancient railroad passenger cars on either side of the road and then turn left on the dirt County Road 831. Stop in the first parking lot on your left near the large black iron

Vindicator Mine headframe. A headframe is a structure built over a vertical mine shaft.

The Hike: Next to the parking lot **(1)** the foreman's house gives us a close up view of what a nicer home of the era was like. The parlor has a respectable fireplace, floral wall paper and an enclosed sun room running the length of the house. Look in all the windows but don't go inside. Typical of an older home, you can see the numerous room additions that have been built over the years. The human touch can be seen in the remnants of the white fence than encircled the front and initials etched into the cement step poured so many decades ago.

Before you start, remember that you are at 10,200 feet elevation. The advice of sunscreen and water is even more important up here. You will be going downhill on the first half so you know that means a slower uphill return. From the parking lot, begin the two mile loop by taking the trail to the right.

Below the large black Vindicator Mine headframe on your right you can see a square of landscaping timbers with a metal grate in the bottom. This is one of the many sealed mine shafts in the area. See if you can spot more along the way as you explore.

The small stone and brick buildings with concrete arched roofs that you will spot along the way were for the storage of dynamite. There is usually a second building not too close by with the blasting caps, wisely kept at a safe distance.

After you pass the District Drainage interpretive sign, look on the other side of the trail **(2),** just below the fence. There are three large metal objects. The signs provide excellent

The blasting caps were kept well away from the dynamite

information, but all the rest of this mysterious rusty equipment is what makes it a good exploration to go along with a good hike. Do you wonder what that huge crescent band is?

The large cable-wound drums seen along the hike were for the mine hoists. For a brake, they used an iron band that would tighten against the drum to stop the hoist from turning. A wooden lining on the band worked like the brake shoes on a car. This curious circle of **(2)** black iron with a piece of wood still attached is just that. You will see more of them in place later on down the trail.

This large ore house **(3)** for the Vindicator Mine originally had a mountain hillside of tailings behind it but these valuable rocks were removed decades later to be reprocessed. On the next bend you will pass through a grove of small pine trees **(4)** that were planted after the stone was removed. Although it is a drop in the (ore) bucket, we appreciate the efforts they made.

It appears that this wooden ore house **(5)** is ready to collapse any minute and that we should wait around with cameras in hand to witness the imminent tumble. Behind this you can visit a low building with a slanted roof that has a whimsical feel to its silhouette although it was built solely for function. An excellent example of an ore tipple **(6)** with rails still in place is on your left.

These three little buildings **(7)** bring the human story to light. The house with the small brick chimney has an antique refrigerator lying out front. The corrugated steel barn has a little hay loft door and a beam above for lifting the hay. Just around the bend in the trail is a third building surrounded by a grove of aspen trees. Low and sturdy with logs outside and angular sawn planks expertly mounted inside, this two room dirt floor building was done well. By the layout and size we can guess this third building may have been an upscale shelter for their donkeys, built with love.

This is the lowest point **(8)** of the loop and it's all uphill from here. There are two groundwater quality monitoring wells that can be seen near the trail.

The little town of Goldfield will be on your right across the highway. See if you can spot the wonderfully preserved firehouse near the upper center of town with its bell tower still in place. Now just a few blocks long, Goldfield was once a mining union town of 3,500 people. Goldfield had a suburb named Hollywood and there was a small town called Los Angeles next to Hollywood.

The heavy stonework **(9)** is the back wall for the LaBella Power Plant that supplied electricity for the interurban trolley system that ran between towns. It's time to head uphill. Above you is the Theresa Mine **(11)** that you drove by earlier. At the junction in the trail **(10)** near the parking lot, cut back to your left to visit the Theresa Mine.

The Theresa Mine is a rare opportunity to legally enter some mine buildings to explore. One building looks like a

The Theresa Mine

warming shed and staging area for the miners prior to their descent into the shaft. The massive iron headframe was built to last. As you continue the hike past the Theresa Mine, you will spot a corrugated tin outhouse **(12)** built on a skid frame sitting above a depression in the tailings above you. Made to be moved as work progresses, this is the oldest porta-potty that you may ever encounter.

74

Follow the short spur in the trail **(13)** to get to the location of the Golden Cycle Mine. Not much is visible but this mine was a big deal back in the day. The Golden Cycle Mill in Colorado Springs is related to this mine. The only visible remnant of the Colorado Springs mill is the smokestack seen from Highway 24 and 21st Street.

More mine bits, more rock **(14)**. The dark coating on the rocks is a patina of desert varnish that appears on exposed rocks in a dry climate. This patina is the same stuff scraped away by some Native Americans to create petroglyphs in other parts of the country.

By this time, **(15)** you will be happy to not only see a bench at the scenic overlook but be relieved that the trail is leveling out. This is a unique view of the backside of the Pikes Peak summit. Take a moment to figure out the information on the sign that is filled with details. Rest your legs and assess how well you managed your water bottle now that you are near the end of the loop. Good hike, good history.

There is a rich selection of roads and trails around the Cripple Creek and Victor area. This Vindicator Valley trail had the benefits of signage but now you know what all this stuff was for. Don't trespass, be safe and go explore more of the Cripple Creek Mining District!

A Step Farther:
Golden memories in Victor

Having made the trip all the way from Colorado Springs to Cripple Creek, go into the nearby historic mining town of Victor. It has been said that in the height of the 1890s Colorado gold rush, Victor's streets were paved with gold. I believe that may be historic remembrance hyperbole. Surely the roads through town were not made of real gold because pickaxe prospecting would then have been too easy, and the streets would have been all torn up again. Just saying. Still, many golden memories are attached to this historic mining town.

Victor officially became a city in 1894 in the height of the gold rush and grew to about 18,000 people. Many of the best gold mines in the region were located above Victor. Between Cripple Creek and the neighboring town of Victor, it is estimated the area produced 21 million ounces of gold, which by today's value would have been worth more than 10 billion dollars. That's a lot of gold to pave streets. Whereas the mine owners and investors lived in Cripple Creek and Colorado Springs, most of the mineworkers lived in Victor. The heavyweight-boxing champ, Jack Dempsey, was a mucker, shoveling broken rock into ore carts in the Portland Mine.

Today's Victor is quiet with few residents, and fewer open businesses but it is a fun, authentic 1890s mining town to visit. The downtown is gradually undergoing rejuvenation with new sidewalks, a sprucing up of the building facades, and newly paved streets (not gold ... dang).   Take a self-guided walking tour of this National Register Historic Business District featuring numerous curbside interpretive signs with photos and information from the Gold Rush Era. Maps and brochures are available around town and the Lowell Thomas Museum.

As if the ruins of a mill and dozens of lovely restored downtown Victorian buildings were not enough to explore, go to the closed Gold Coin Mine right in the center of town, and read about how they wove their own unique flat steel cable. The problem was that the edges of the flat cable would fray against the drum but found a repurpose as guard rails along the hilly roads in the area.

A gold vein was discovered during construction of a hotel foundation in the center of Victor so the solution of course was to forget about the hotel, keep digging and open a mine! The big challenge was where to place the Gold Coin Mine's tailings. The solution was to build a 3,700 foot tunnel to the valley below town just to remove the rock debris.

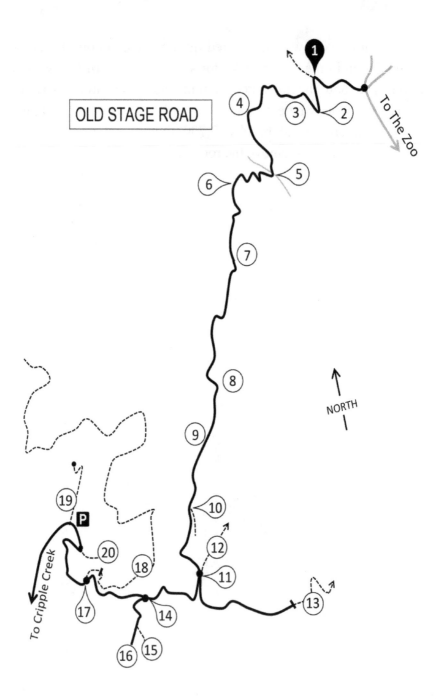

OLD STAGE ROAD

To The Zoo

NORTH

To Cripple Creek

7

Old Stage Road

A driving exploration in a hiking book

A driving exploration? "But wait, this is a hiking book," you say. Let us explain! This steep, winding, narrow dirt road is the back road to the Gold Camp Road and a fun way to get to the mining district of Cripple Creek and Victor. We are willing to bet that we can show you several hikes and points of interest along the way that you did not know about and isn't that what this book is all about?

The route began as a simple path called the Cheyenne Mountain Trail traveling to the west flank of Pikes Peak. The trail grew into a lumber road before gold was discovered in Cripple Creek in 1858. Once gold was found, it turned into a wagon and stage road. At one time it was even being groomed as an alternate route to Cañon City. The Stage Road then became a toll road in the late 1800s with the tollbooth quite close to where the Broadmoor Hotel now stands, at the intersection of Penrose Boulevard and Alta Vista Lane. Is it just us or do other people wonder when it changed from Stage Road to Old Stage Road?

This Old Stage Road is also known as Forest Service Road 368 (FS 368). Hiking or biking on this road is discouraged due to the steep narrow grade and the traffic that you will encounter along this dirt road (see **A Drive Farther** below). If you are hiking or biking to the Gold Camp Road, start on the closed portion of the Gold Camp Road, found elsewhere in this book.

First of all, a heads up. We see regular cars up there all the time; you do not need a high clearance, four-wheel drive vehicle, but it is a dirt road typically with washboards, pot holes and ruts that can be quite bad at times. If driving this road does not feel right to you, keep in mind that it will not get any better until you hit the junction with Gold Camp Road six miles later at the top. Helen Hunt Jackson said it best: "The road tacks as sharply as a ship in a gale...."

DISTANCE - 6 MILES ONE WAY

DRIVE TO TRAILHEADS

ELEVATION GAIN – 3,000 FEET

Getting There: To begin, head for the Cheyenne Mountain Zoo. The Old Stage Road is accessed from Penrose Boulevard at the four-way stop sign just below the Cheyenne Mountain Zoo. Take Old Stage Road uphill through the picturesque residential neighborhood until you hit a switchback with a large bank of mailboxes **(1)**. To the right of the mailboxes is a connection to the Chamberlain Trail that leads to South Cheyenne Canyon entrance and to Seven Falls. In the future, the Chamberlain Trail will span the Front Range for the full length of Colorado Springs. Only short pieces are completed now but it has been in the city's master plan for over 100 years. Several hiking options will be identified along this exploration and we will point out trailheads but will not walk you through them as we have a drive to accomplish!

At the next switchback, the paved road turns to dirt (2). This is where your real wilderness adventure begins! At this switchback, set your odometer to zero. Your very first turn on the dirt road (3) is a blind corner crowded by a rock outcropping. This is a good place to remind you to watch for the weekend Jeep crowd racing up and down the road as it accesses some quality mountain off road trails.

0.2 At the pullout just around the corner, look up beyond the power lines to see an old wooden aqueduct carrying an iron water supply pipeline. This piece of 1926 pipe is still in use, but most of this water line was replaced in 1934. You will spot remnants along the way.

0.8 On your left is the Sunrise Trail, on private property. On your right is a gate (4) and steep road that goes down to one of the Seven Falls' Soaring Adventures zip line courses. Neither of these locations are accessible to the general public, so pass on by.

1.3 The Theater in the Mountains—this is worth a stop. We're driving but we are not in a hurry, right? Find where the road makes a switchback turn (5) as it passes over a valley. There are two truck size boulders next to a small active stream. Back in simpler days there were performances held on summer weekends at this sharp switchback in the road. The performers would use the road as their stage with the valley below as the idyllic backdrop. (No Jeeps on the road back then.) The audience would sit on the hillside above the road to your left. Stop, get out of your car and experience the feel of what that weekend tradition would have been like. (Again, watch for other vehicle traffic.) A short exploration up the valley by the tiny seasonal stream is refreshing.

1.7 The spectacular Soaring Adventures Zip Lines begin **(6)** behind this gate. You may not access them from here, but must purchase tickets (844-876-4968) and be shuttled up from a point near the Golden Bee Pub on Lake Avenue. At the end of your zip line adventure, your party will be shuttled from Seven Falls back to your car.

2.2 This odometer reading marks the Wade Place. On your left you will see a stone wall **(7)** with stone steps next to the road. Above these steps were a cluster of buildings know as Wade's Half Way House. It is not anywhere near half way, by

the way. Around the next bend you can see a fireplace and foundation plus a couple of restored buildings, now a private residence. As an explorer of local history, this place will interest you in a couple of ways. Helen Hunt Jackson mentioned this when documenting her travels, stating that she was impressed by the building (still standing) and by the large boulder to its right. Even more interesting is that Mr. Wade was the grandfather of Fred Barr, the founder of Barr Trail up the face of Pikes Peak. On very early maps of the area, this location is actually marked as Wade. At a right bend in the road **(8)** an area now blocked with boulders shows evidence that it once was a picnic ground next to the creek.

Continuing on, to your right **(9)** is a kiosk with forest service maps and regulations. Just beyond, on your left **(10),** is an access road that parallels the historic water line.

At **4.9** miles you encounter **(11)** Forest Service Road 369, also called Transmitter Way. There is a lot to tell you about at this little intersection, so you can forget about watching your odometer from this point on. The family-run Old Stage Riding Stables at this intersection has an Old West Town design and an assortment of quality forest trails. Their guided horse rides are open to the public (719-448-0371).

At this same intersection, the McNeill Trail **(12)** leads to the location of the old Cheyenne Mountain Lodge, now the home to The Broadmoor Hotel's Cloud Camp on the north summit. The unmarked start of this trail is at the rise in the Old Stage Road just before this intersection. The trail starts to your left, almost horizontal, behind the Stage Stop sign. The first three miles are on public land and may be explored, but plan on being stopped by a Private Property sign for an anti-climactic ending and turnaround quite close to the summit. Although this moderate trail, with fabulous views, goes to the top of the mountain, the Old Stage Road has already done most of the climbing for you, thus providing a gradual grade for this six mile round trip hike.

Still at the same intersection **(11)** by the Old State Riding Stables is Transmitter Way, the road to the left of the stables. Have you wondered how they get to the transmission towers that you see on top of Cheyenne Mountain? You found it! It is no secret because the name of the road is Transmitter Way but it still feels like a valuable find. You may drive the first public mile of this side road before reaching a locked gate. Beyond this gate **(13)** is a rugged unpaved road of zigzags to the antenna farm on the summit. The U.S. Cycling Team used this very challenging road for a training routine in the 1980s. Although the gate feels you may be near the summit, it is actually several more miles to the top. If you really want to go to the top of the mountain, the Dixon Trail in Cheyenne Mountain State Park will take you to the summit near the antenna farm. Climbing the eastern face of Cheyenne Mountain, the Dixon Trail is a challenging 16.5-mile round trip trail with 3,000 feet of tough elevation gain.

Back on Old Stage Road, continue uphill to an intersection with **(14)** Forest Service Road 371. This side road leads to several adventure options. On your left about 3/10 of a mile is a parking area for the unmarked trailhead **(15)** to Grayback Peak. This 3.3 miles long (r/t) climb up Grayback Peak is worth it for the views, including a bird's eye view of the historic Emerald Valley Ranch (private property)—called Camp Vigil back in the mid-1920s. The trail starts out easy at first but gets tougher with a scramble near the top. (Look up to your right from the parking lot for a dramatic view of Mt. Vigil.)

Another 3/10 of a mile will take you to the Pipeline Trail **(16)** on the right that has its very own chapter in this book. At the end of FS 371 is the trailhead to Nanny's Cabin that you will read about in the Pipeline Trail chapter.

Let us get back to the Old Stage Road because the end is now tantalizingly close and we and have more hiking trails ahead. Back on Old Stage Road, continue uphill one half mile to the intersection **(17)** with the Gold Camp Road (FS 370) and the end of the Old Stage Road. You will appreciate how level the old railroad bed is after ascending the steep winding Old Stage Road.

At this intersection, left goes to Cripple Creek and right goes to a nearby tunnel. Turn right for a few hundred feet on this lesser road to end at the collapsed tunnel **(18)** that closed this end of the "Closed Portion of the Gold Camp Road" as seen in another chapter of this book. At this gate, you can hike or bike downhill to the intersection, approximately 8 miles to Helen Hunt Falls. Just remember it is a gentle 2% grade uphill back to this starting place. About a mile into your exploration hike on the closed portion, you will reach a train tunnel in perfect condition. In the spring, look for Mount Rosa Cascade on the other side of tunnel, a tall waterfall of melting snow.

Back to your car. If you go left at the junction **(17)**, you will be on The Gold Camp Road to Cripple Creek.

Even if you do not plan to continue the 30 miles to Cripple Creek, it will add to your adventure to drive a short 8/10 of a mile to the St. Peter's Dome overlook **(19)** before you turn around. You will experience a unique view of the city from this parking area and the trail to St Peter's Dome is a scenic one. Down the narrow dirt road on the right of the overlook's parking lot is another collapsed train tunnel. You will also find **(20)** diggings for fluorite, a purple mineral.

The railroad bed gets confusing in this area as the train's serpentine track took 2 miles to gain elevation in this area while the road takes a third of that. The road to St Peter's Dome actually uses the train bed in the reverse direction for a bit. Don't try to figure it out, just enjoy the exploration.

We struggle with the decision at this point; do we continue the longer drive to Cripple Creek's restaurants and slot machines or take the quick washboard route back down? Your call!

A Drive Farther:
Don't get clobbered

Part or this adventure involves *not* getting hit head-on by a 4-wheel-drive vehicle flying around a blind curve. (We are not trying to be over-alarming, just expressing caution.) El Paso County deliberately leaves this Old Stage Road rough (although okay for low-clearance sedans) to try to keep the "indestructible" Jeep crowd from speeding on this wilderness road with ruts, pot holes and teeth-rattling washboard areas. Still, every year, someone runs off the edge, going too fast for road or weather conditions.

Take it slow—you are in no hurry for your discoveries anyway. Stay alert for oncoming traffic, especially on busy summer weekends. It is kind of fun looking at all the souped-up Jeeps driving to areas deeper into the mountains to test their worthiness on branch, off-road vehicle trails. We just don't want too close of an encounter.

Old Stage Road

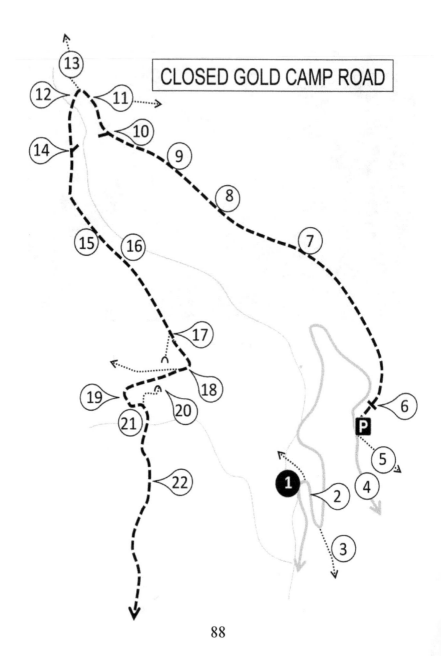

CLOSED GOLD CAMP ROAD

8
Closed Gold Camp Road

*The mother trail to
so many other trails*

The Gold Camp Road was once a railroad bed for the train that hauled the ore from Cripple Creek mines to the mills in Colorado Springs. In the 1920s, the rails were removed, the 31 wooden trestles were filled in with mine tailings and an auto road was built.

In 1989, a seven mile portion of the Gold Camp Road was permanently closed due to two tunnel cave-ins. They reopened the road for a bit and the tunnels did what old tunnels do, again, so the road was closed for good. Fortunately for us all, these unusable tunnels turned into a hiking goldmine.

This hike is on a very gradual incline as dictated by the mountain railroad's abilities and this stretch is the access to numerous public hiking trails in the foothills area. Starting just above Helen Hunt Falls, this closed roadbed will easily take you to the Seven Bridges Trail and St. Mary's Falls Trail, but the trail has attractions of its own. In addition to the two tunnels that are gated there are two more tunnels in perfect shape along the 8.5 miles of lightly used roadbed for the adventuresome. On this hike we are only going to experience the first 2 miles in this chapter and the first of the gated tunnels.

We suggest going early in the day during the busy summer months as this is a hub to multiple trails and can be full by midday. The experience is pretty exposed, so remember sunscreen and lots of water.

Getting There: From Old Colorado City, take 21st Street south. It will change names to Cresta Avenue. Turn right on to Cheyenne Boulevard. (You may also access Cheyenne Boulevard from South Tejon Street.)

Cheyenne Boulevard will take you directly to the North Cheyenne Canyon. At the entrance to North Cheyenne Cañon is a picturesque stone house called the Starsmore Discovery Center with hiking trail maps and information.

(See: www.cheyennecanon.org—Note that there is no Y in the Spanish spelling of canyon.) It is well worth the stop for a trail map of the area and the knowledge of the staff. This parking lot is also the starting point to the Columbine Trail that ends at Helen Hunt Falls and to the Stratton Open Space's numerous loop trails.

Fun fact: This stone house once stood at the northwest corner of East Cheyenne Road and South Nevada Avenue. The story of the stone house and Mary's trees are in **A Step Farther** below.

Begin your drive up the winding paved road in North Cheyenne Cañon. This streamside drive up a steep and narrow granite valley is an adventure in itself. North Cheyenne Cañon is an excellent road to take your out-of-town guests to experience "the mountains" so close to town. There are streamside picnic grounds and picturesque stone bridges. The Stratton Open Space, Columbine Trail, Mount Cutler Trail and the Mount Muscoco Trail start here from points in this valley, but as they say, wait, there's more!

Stop at Helen Hunt Falls **(1)** for a short warmup hike on the trail to the Silver Cascade Falls. The outhouses in the parking lot are the last official restrooms for today. On the road just beyond Helen Hunt Falls look for the stone retaining wall **(2)** with BRUIN INN inlaid in quartz, a reminder of a business that burned down a century ago. Soon after that you will spot the sign for the upper end to the Columbine Trail **(3)** that started at the Starsmore building at the base of the canyon.

One more switchback will take you to the large gravel parking lot (Pull Off 18) that will be the start of today's hike. Look across the valley at the straight horizontal cut in the trees to see where you will soon be hiking.

Water tank **(8)** and trestle **(10)** & **(14)**
Photo from 1970s US Forest Service Brochure

The road to your right **(4)** is the drivable portion of the Lower Gold Camp Road that will take you down to Old Colorado City and the gold mill locations that were the destination of the ore trains from the Cripple Creek District. This road will take you through Tunnel Number One and Tunnel Number Two.

The gated road in the middle **(5)** is the High Drive, recently closed to vehicle traffic; it is an alternate road to Old Colorado City and is hiking/biking access to the popular Captain Jack's Trail. The gated road to your left at the back of the parking lot **(6)** is the closed portion of the Gold Camp Road and the trailhead for your hike today.

The railroad's water tower foundation **(8)**

The hike: Pass through the gate and follow the road. In less than a half mile, on your right, there is a small prospector's tunnel **(7)** in the hillside next to the road that looks like a prospector's dig. Note the narrow vertical vein of dark matter above that would encourage such a prospect. It's hard to spot going this direction. If you miss it, you'll see it easier coming back down. The tunnel is small in diameter and does not go very deep, but without a bright flashlight, it looks intriguing!

Look for three concrete blocks (**8**) next to a gulley on your right. These are the remnants of a water tower for the steam powered railroad engines. The water was supplied by Cheyenne Creek which you will soon encounter.

On your right is the base of the sign (**9**) from Pike National Forest from the days when it was the road to Cripple Creek.

Only the base remains

Just past the sign, look for the stub of the road on your left (**10**) jutting out. The creek can be seen and heard below. This was once the start of a high timber trestle for the U turn to continue the climb across the valley. The trestle was removed and now the road makes a sharp turn as it crosses the stream just ahead.

On your right is a well-worn trail (**11**) that connects to the Seven Bridges Trail. It actually connects to the Buckhorn Cutoff Trail. Don't take this spur as you will miss the first bridge and a much prettier beginning to the Seven Bridges hike. Next to Cheyenne Creek you will spot a sign (**12**) for Trail 622, the real Seven Bridges Trailhead. We don't take you there on this hike but Seven Bridges (**13**) is one of the more beautiful hikes in the canyon and can get busy at times. It is a three mile round trip with 600 feet of elevation gain and of course, seven bridges. If you'd like, the trail continues after the seventh bridge, taking the hiker to open hillsides with great views of Cheyenne Creek and Colorado Springs below, to the aspen-ringed Jones Park, and on to the intersection of the Captain Jack Trail (one could do a whole loop hike back to the parking lot, if so ambitious).

Back to our hike. As the road makes a sharp bend to the left you will be starting up the opposite side of the valley. The other end of the trestle that bypassed the sharp turn juts to the left **(14)** but is harder to spot than the one on the other side of the stream. On the right hand side is a treeless hillside of decomposed granite pebbles and round boulders **(15)**. The city harvested the large round boulders that had rolled down over the years for the landscaping around the building and base of Helen Hunt Falls. Very convenient! Looking up—you can see that more boulders could make themselves available soon. Much of our erosion is caused by the freeze and thaw. As the melting snow refreezes and expands the pebbles will loosen and then the spring rains will set them free.

On the left is a tall retaining wall **(16)** that keeps the road in place and protects the camp buildings that you can see below. Just beyond, on your right, is a BLM survey marker. We don't know if you will be interested, but we get excited over these little finds.

Your trail will veer to the left to go up over the closed tunnel and the road ends **(17)** as it runs into Tunnel Number 3. As you peer through the gate on this end of the tunnel you can see the tunnel is not fully collapsed but you can also understand by the fallen stone why it is not safe. Notice the soot on the roof that came from the steam engines? Take the trail up and over the tunnel.

Exiting the tunnel went immediately to a trestle
Photograph by Stewarts Commercial Photographers,
© Pikes Peak Library District 013-8463

Above the tunnel you will see an uphill fork **(18)** in the trail to St. Mary's Falls. You are 1.2 miles from your car and the trail to the falls is 1.6 miles one way with a 1,100 foot elevation gain. This trail is steeper and longer than the Seven Bridges Trail but the cool water and the city view from the waterfall are the rewards for your hike. Again, we don't take you to St. Mary's Falls in this chapter, so continue on around the tunnel, ford the small stream **(19)** and find a tiny but picturesque trailside waterfall behind a rock wall and the other end of the tunnel.

When the railroad was operational, exiting this tunnel **(20)** was said to be a bit of a thrill, as it pops out of the dark tunnel directly onto a high trestle. There are no signs of the trestle remaining but you can envision a straight line from the tunnel's portal to the road bed **(21)** ahead. Look back at the tunnel exit

95

from the road to see that the hillside on the right is one large slippery granite slab that has the tunnel bore and continues on

Tunnel number three as it appears today **(20)**

down to the Silver Cascade Falls below. There is no connecting trail from here to the waterfalls below.

This is a good point to turn around **(22)**. From this point on, the road continues for another six miles through two more tunnels and then to another gated tunnel at the intersection of Old Stage Road and the open portion of Gold Camp Road. These 5 miles of closed roadbed are a gradual 2% incline but there is not much more to point out other than miles of isolated mountain scenery. If you choose to go another mile, the road will soon go around a sharp curve and the views of Cheyenne Mountain and Fort Carson will appear. The wide spot in the road was called Fairview Siding where the helper engine was staged to assist trains over the mountain pass on the way to the gold camps. You can learn more about the other end of this closed road in the Old Stage Road chapter.

A Step Farther:
Mary had a little house

As you first enter North Cheyenne Cañon to access several hiking trails, or to visit Helen Hunt Falls with its adjoining log cabin nature center, you will see a beautiful stone building on your left—one that looks more like a house than a visitor center building. And in fact, it once was a home, and not originally at this location!

The Starsmore Discovery Center stone house once stood at the northwest corner of Cheyenne Road and South Nevada Avenue in Colorado Springs. That location is now a McDonald's restaurant ... more on that in a moment.

In 1992, the city of Colorado Springs bought the Starsmore family home and moved it to its present canyon location at the gateway to beautiful rock formations, waterfalls, wildlife and wildflowers. Today at the Discovery Center—also called the Starsmore Nature and Visitor Center—guests of all ages can acquire free canyon maps, learn regional history, see fun dioramas and hands-on nature exhibits, as well as get information on guided hikes and children's nature programs.

Jim and Mary Starsmore loved the stone house that he built in 1928. If you visit the parking lot of that McDonalds on the corner of East Cheyenne Road and South Nevada Avenue, you will see some of the original 35 juniper trees that were planted in 1918 on the property perimeter—today not as neatly manicured as in the days of the original owners. Mary could often be seen with a sunbonnet on, clippers in hand, climbing a tall step ladder and carefully trimming and sculpting each 35-foot tall, slender tree around her home.

But Mary's legacy didn't end there. When Mary passed, she left her remaining estate in an endowed fund that would forever care for this beloved community asset. Today, the Friends of Cheyenne Cañon maintain the Starsmore Discovery Center with the $25,000 annual gift that comes from Mary's estate.

Mary Starsmore was a proper lady but she didn't hesitate climbing up a tall ladder to groom her beloved juniper trees. And then there was Captain Jack, a true frontier woman.

Another Step Farther:
The dude was a lady

Near the trailhead of the closed portion to Gold Camp Road is a trailhead (really a whole interconnected trail system) in North Cheyenne Cañon: Captain Jack's Trail. These linked and intersecting trails can be combined for loops, extra mileage, and more adventure. Some of these additional explorations include trails like Seven Bridges, Loud's Cabin, High Drive, and the Pipeline Trail.

But who was Captain Jack? Most folks that hike this trail probably have no idea that Captain Jack was Ellen E. Jack, a woman. And what an interesting woman she was!

Captain Jack was born in England in 1842; she and her first husband arrived in America just before the Civil War. After the war ended, she moved to Pueblo, to Denver, then to Colorado Springs in 1903. She was a tough, gun-toting woman who spent years wandering around Colorado, took part in gunfights with bandits, "fought off 'amorous' Indians" (according to her autobiography, *The Fate of a Fairy*), was part owner of a successful mine, and traveled through avalanche-prone mountain passes where others couldn't.

High Drive became her home and she opened up wild-west tourist cabins and a resort on her property, leading burro rides and posing for photos with her gun, pet cats and parrots. Captain Jack died in 1921 and was buried in Evergreen Cemetery with her gravestone facing High Drive and the Rockies.

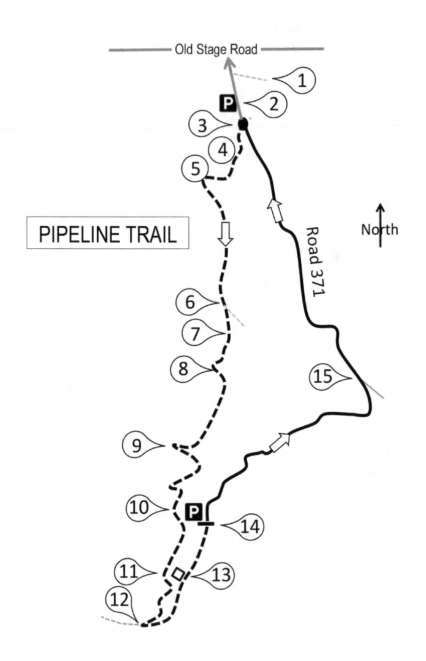

9
The Pipeline Trail

The little pipe that grew a great resort

I have always had an interest in pipeline trails. They are typically easy to follow with minimal ups and downs, allowing gravity to do the work of moving the water. My curiosity about the history of a pipeline frequently results in explorations that involve a hike. Where does the pipe come from, how and when was it built, and where does it go? I actually *hope* it involves a hike! The name "Pipeline Trail" comes from a utilitarian

Distance: 5 Mile Loop
Difficulty: 🌲🌲🌲🌲🌲
Elevation Gain: 500 ft

installation. Although they are frequently built across public land these trails weren't meant to be for the public, yet they turned out to be a boon to us all. Every state has them and there has been no need to change their names to something more exciting or romantic. They are typically a dirt path on top of the buried pipe. Functional made fun. I know of three public accessible pipeline trails just in the Pikes Peak Region alone. One is on the side of nearby Mt. Rosa (the mountain that Zebulon Pike was suspected to have summited; not the one that bears his name today). A second pipeline trail is running from the lakes that are seen from the cog train and terminates at the hydroelectric power plant by the cog train depot. (The Mount Manitou Incline was initially built for the installation of this pipeline as described in the "Above The Incline" chapter.)

For the sake of this chapter we are only interested in the third Pipeline Trail that starts high off of Old Stage Road. This Pipeline Trail follows the Rosemont Reservoir pipeline, still in use today although the pipe is delivering at a reduced capacity due to its age. This loop hike is 2.5 miles on the trail with another 1.5 miles back on the Forest Service road to the start.

First, a quick story of the origin of this little pipeline: Spencer Penrose's luxury hotel in the Wild West was an equally wild success from the day it opened in June of 1918. The Broadmoor Hotel at the base of the Rockies drew visitors from all over the country and around the world. The region grew and Penrose kept building. The elegant guests, the grand fountain in front of the hotel and the Broadmoor lake itself had created a demand for water, as did the polo field and private residences with prestigious landscaping that began to surround the property. Penrose also wanted to make sure his new golf course would stay green in the summer months but he foresaw that the local infrastructure would not handle the growth. Penrose bought the Rosemont area in the mountains above for one million dollars to obtain the water rights. He ran a 10-inch diameter waterline for 12 miles from the dam at the Rosemont Reservoir down to a tiny reservoir above the Broadmoor golf course. In 1932, once that water became available, it was time to grow again. He bought over 2,000 more acres near the hotel for a development to be called Broadmoor Heights. A second polo field was added to the operation. This purchase also included much of the eastern face of Cheyenne Mountain where the zoo is now located. All of that expansion and development was due, in no small part, to this lowly little pipeline laid through a lush canyon to the base of the mountains. The ultimate destination of this pipeline is a small reservoir below the Cheyenne Mountain Zoo. From inside the zoo you can spot the Penrose Reservoir just below the gate entrance.

This pipeline trail is a pleasant hike with a little of everything for everyone. You will traverse through thickly forested areas, go by natural rock formations and manmade retaining walls of granite boulders, cross a small stream and view a picturesque waterfall, pass by openings in the pines to observe and enjoy panoramic vistas, and then end up at an aspen encircled meadow with cabin ruins in its center. Along the way, you will see historical artifacts related to the original pipeline and trail, including more exposed original pipe, retaining walls, stone bridges, ancient manholes, and more. Eighty years ago, the pipeline was protected with walls of expertly laid boulders and covered with earth. It is impressive how well these structures that you will be walking on have held up.

Getting There: Take Lake Avenue to the roundabout in front of the Broadmoor and then go left on the roundabout for a pretty drive between golf courses. At the four-way stop intersection, continue straight ahead on Old Stage Road. Your adventure begins when you leave Old Stage Road's asphalt and start up the nearly 150 year old historic Stagecoach Road. See the "Old Stage Road" chapter. Approximately six miles up Old Stage Road, turn left on Forest Service Road 371. Watch for horses on the road and yield right-of-way.

(1) After 1/4 mile on 371, watch on your left for a pullout capable of holding several cars. This is the parking area for the trail to the top of Grayback Peak, a beautiful hike, but it is a more aggressive adventure than you will be doing today. Keep going.

(2) Continue another 200 yards down the road to a small pullout on the right. This is your starting point. Park here and walk down the road a very short distance to a pullout on the right just big enough for one car, but don't be tempted to park here as horses will occasionally access this location.

(3) The trailhead has no sign but is marked appropriately by a section of pipeline that has been exposed over time. (After the hike, you will be walking back along this dirt road to return to your car.)

The Hike: Begin by walking up the trail along the exposed pipe. Stay on the trail and obey the No Trespassing signs. This first part of the trail is along private land.

(4) Within a very short walk you will see the remains of a fluorite mine tipple and a tailings mound on the right. Tipple is a fun word to say, isn't it? A mine tipple is usually constructed of heavy timbers and looks like an unfinished bridge. The mine cars would be pushed from the mine to the end of the wooden tipple's elevated iron rail to dump the unwanted rock. Curiously, this mine, called the Timberline Tunnel, is at an elevation of 8,500 feet, about 3,000 feet below actual timberline.

Fluorite is a purple mineral used for iron processing and you will see mine tailings that have plenty of purple veined rock to kick around, but it is never wise to enter a mine area itself. Fluorite was discovered here in 1883 and a mine operated at this location from 1910-1918. The mine briefly reopened for the war effort in 1944-1945. The 800 foot horizontal mine bore has since been sealed due to a collapse of the entrance.

After you pass the mine you will spot a private residence to the left of the trail. This property was homesteaded in 1909 and is still family owned. Keep going and respect their privacy. You will spot, just across their fence, a natural spring that surfaces for their water supply.

(5) Continue following the pipeline trail uphill on the gentle climb. About ¼ mile from the mine tailings you will encounter a small waterfall and cross a short wooden foot

A cut that was dynamited in the ridge for the pipeline
created a nice pass for hikers today

bridge that spans the first of several streams, some wet, some dry. Immediately after the bridge is a weathered but well executed sign designating an intersecting side trail to Bear Trap Ranch. Continue straight ahead.

All along this route on the right side of the trail you will see pieces of a short retaining wall. Instead of trying to trench into the hard granite mountain, it appears that the pipe was laid on the ground and then covered with soil held back by this retaining wall. Smart.

(6) In approximately ½ mile you will encounter a fork in the trail. Keep right. The left fork is a horse trail that leads back to the road, but go right, the good stuff is ahead. Carry on, intrepid explorer.

(7) Quickly after this split in the trail you will run across an ingenious design to keep the pipe from washing out as it crosses a gulley. It looks like a dam with an underpass and that's pretty much what it is. The pipeline is protected by this stone structure and there is a square tunnel built to let the water from the upper gully flow below the buried pipeline. Not far beyond, keep your eyes open for a nice view of Greyback Peak across the valley to your left.

(8) Three hundred yards ahead, you will encounter a cut that has been dynamited out of the granite. Just like the roadways in our mountainous state, this notch was created to level out the pipeline and it turned out to be convenient for hikers, too. Envision the original surface of the ridgeline.

(9) In the next gulley, watch for a large manhole cover with an open pipe extending out of the side into a dry creek bed. This piece of exposed pipe is my favorite discovery on the hike. A fascinating find in the middle of the woods reinforces what we already know about Spencer Penrose. Inside this manhole is a valve to release water from the pipeline so that it may gush down this gulley, hijacking the flow of the water for his personal ponds at his ranch. If Penrose wanted water in his lovely ponds, he got water.

(10) As you continue your hike down the trail, watch for the first in a series of square concrete pads. The pipeline is encased inside of a cube of concrete.

I can't help but to speculate as to why these heavy blocks of concrete are along this stretch and nowhere else along the line that we have seen. Did they learn that they didn't need them as the water rushed downhill lower in the valley? Is the ground unstable enough here to need the extra control? Are they concerned that the freeze/thaw cycles may lift the pipe over time? I remind myself to quit overthinking it and enjoy the hike.

Watch for evidence of several tiny leaks from the 80-year-old pipeline seeping to the surface. You will also spot some modern patches that have been applied as proof that this pipeline may be replaced in the next decade. Fortunately, the trail will persevere.

(11) Find the concrete block that has initials and the date of May 13, 1932 written in the concrete. Not long after this block, look down through the pines to your left for the first view of the stone fireplace and foundation of Nanny's Cabin. You will be passing this area very soon on your way back down.

(12) Just a bit farther along you will see where the trail joins a dirt road. Turn left on this road towards the ruins of Nanny's Cabin. Thus begins your return via the dirt road to your starting point.

If you were to continue up the valley, and I don't recommend it, you would find the head of this pipeline below the dam for the Rosemont Reservoir but this would create an additional 8 miles of hiking round trip on a rustic trail. A city water supply and fishing spot today, this reservoir can be easily reached from the Gold Camp Road. To drive to the base of the dam and the origin of this pipeline, take County Road 372 off of the Gold Camp Road. It has been said that Theodore Roosevelt once hunted game on this land during his presidency.

(13) Okay, back to the hike. Who was Nanny, and what's the story of her cabin? I'm glad you asked. Nanny (yes, there was a real nanny) would entertain the children while the adults

The fireplace still stands at Nanny's Cabin

partied at Spencer Penrose's ranch down below. Read more of her story in **A Step Farther** at the end of this chapter. A good amount of the historic cabin's concrete foundation still exists, as well as the building's photogenic stone fireplace and chimney. Find the large campfire ring behind the cabin. Can you picture the kids singing songs around a large bonfire while a more grown up party livened up the night in the valley below?

Tim and I first discussed our future book among these ruins of the past. After your visit to the cabin in the meadow, continue on down the road. This road parallels a beautiful stream and will take you back to your starting point. Don't be surprised if you startle a wild turkey, quail or mule deer along the way.

(14) In approximately 1/2 mile, you will encounter a gate across the road and the farthest point that the public may drive on Forest Service Road 371. After another half mile and you pass the **(15)** private entrance of Emerald Valley Ranch. Continue along the road one last mile to your car.

A **Step Farther:**
Little cabin in the meadow

As you near the completion of the Pipeline Trail portion of this exploration—at about the halfway point of your adventure—you will encounter the ruins of Nanny's Cabin. You will not want to miss an elevated view from the trail looking down from the forest into this part of Emerald Valley on what's left of the building set in the midst of aspens and wildflowers, but the trail directions will take you right to the ruins. As you walk around much of what is left of the old log cabin stone foundation and the fireplace and chimney, imagine what this setting was like in the early 20th century.

Back in the mid-1920s, Spencer Penrose (the founder of the Broadmoor Hotel) and a few buddies bought the property that is now Emerald Valley Ranch. The 17 acres of campground, cabins, and the surrounding land were once a lumber mill and subsequently, a Girl Scout camp. The Penrose group purchased the camp, renamed it Camp Vigil (Spanish: vee-hil) after the prominent rock formation you saw as you entered at the top of the valley off Old Stage Road. They turned the property into a private hunting camp, however, some speculate that there was more drinking (during the time of prohibition!) and cigar smoking going on than any actual hunting.

Penrose and his wife Julie would bring as many as 100 guests up to Camp Vigil for a night of dining and dancing ... with a full orchestra! After dinner, the children would be taken by horse and buggy to Nanny's Cabin to be watched by Nanny for the balance of the evening while the parents enjoyed the rest of their time. (It was rumored, too, that Penrose didn't care much for kids, so that may have been another reason for their evacuation from camp.)

What's left of the ruins of Nanny's Cabin today provides just a limited view back in time. Divided, broken, stone foundations suggest one larger room with smaller side rooms (bedrooms?), along with what might have been a kitchen. Mounds around the cabin may have been a leach field, outhouses or a dump site. Other, more recent concrete foundations and flooring with drains are evidence that boys' and girls' showers were added for a later camp when Penrose sold the property. With a little more exploring, you might find more to the story of this nearly hidden past.

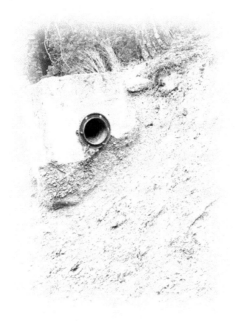

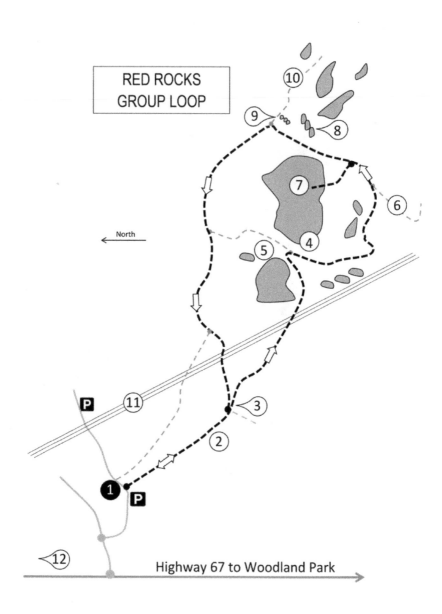

RED ROCKS
GROUP LOOP

North

Highway 67 to Woodland Park

10

Red Rocks Group Trail and Manitou Park

But not those Red Rocks
and not in Manitou Springs

So far in this book we have been enjoying spotting mankind's remnants of the past as an excuse to get outside and hike. Mother Nature supplies the remnants on this hike. No ranches, mines, bridges or railroads. The red rocks on this loop have an ancient story to tell along this in-and-out walk with a loop at the end that is the lollypop on the map.

Yes, this is another Red Rocks park; is that four or five? These red rocks are much smaller than the other Red Rocks parks in the state and Manitou Park is not near Manitou Springs, but the two locations share a logical tie.

Doctor William Bell was an associate of General William Palmer. While Palmer founded Colorado Springs in 1871, Dr. Bell created Manitou Springs a year later.

The same year that he founded Manitou Springs, Dr. Bell purchased 10,000 acres of land a few miles north of Woodland Park with the idea of creating a resort named Manitou Park, and the intent of tying together the two vacation destinations. Nearby is Manitou Lake. Until we started researching this chapter, we had always wondered why Manitou Lake was not near Manitou Springs. To make it more confusing, Woodland Park was initially called Manitou Park, but that has nothing to do with Dr. Bell.

Getting there: The scenic mountain town of Woodland Park is 17 miles west of Colorado Springs on Highway 24. After passing through Woodland Park, turn north on Highway 67. Three and one half miles north of town, turn right on County Road 335, at the Red Rocks Group Campground sign.

Distance: 1 to 2 miles
Difficulty: ♠
Elev. Gain: minimal

One half mile on this dirt road will take you to the campground on the left and your trail parking on the right.

The hike: From the closest parking lot, go through the old log fence **(1)** on the trail marked 708. As you ascend, keep your eyes open for some stonework **(2)** crossing the drainage. Decades old and no longer effective, they were placed to stem the erosion on the trail that goes up the gulley. You may also spot in this area a series of log posts set in a line. Now in a forested area, we are guessing they may have been a boundary for a parking area at one time.

The trail forks in this area. Take the middle fork towards the large red sandstone formation on the left. Walk to the right of the formation **(3)**, staying close to the rock, as you will be circling the grouping in a counter-clockwise direction.

We propose that you not just follow our route, but that you explore the area's hiding places, caves, slides and slopes. There are car and house size boulders sitting alone in the tress, waiting to be found. Wander the formations and explore the trails but keep your bearings. There is a power line **(11)** running through the area that crosses over the parking lot. As long as you are aware of that power line, you won't get lost.

At the first gap between the large formations **(4)** this is an excellent place to climb the rocks and explore the crevices. Or just sit on top quietly and enjoy the scenic setting.

Three Sisters and a Child

A trail traverses this gap **(5)** that will connect with the trail back down, but we don't want to go back yet, we just got started. This hike can be as short or as long as you want. We say "who is counting"?

As you pass to the right of these boulders, follow the trail that appears to leave the area and head towards the power lines. There is a trail junction **(6)** on the right that leads to some smaller boulders but will dead end. Take the left fork to round the back of the largest formation. As you pass around the end of the formation, watch for an area that leads up onto the **(7)** middle of the

115

formation. From here, follow the trail downhill. Just as you start down, look over your right shoulder. There is a formation of three large pillars **(8)** and a smaller one in front that fuels the imagination. Amazingly, to the left of that, (still on your right) is another set **(9)** of three pillars, shorter this time. At this point, you will intersect a trail. To the left is back down to your start. To your right **(10)** the trail leaves the rock formations and ascends through the trees. There is no specific destination, but it is a good way to extend your hike out and back if you wish.

Although it is called a lollypop trail, there are countless unmarked trails lacing the area and if you want to make it a spaghetti trail, go for it!

Manitou Park: After the hike, we would like to surprise you with a visit to a nearby historic site. Return to Highway 67 and turn right. Drive a quick three miles north **(12)** to cross over some wetlands with beaver dams and continue past Manitou Lake. (Manitou Lake requires a small state park fee, but it is worth the visit. Lakeside picnic tables and fishing spots make for a serene scene as you circle the lake on the well maintained trail. This lake was originally built for the tourists visiting Manitou Park.)

Soon after you pass the lake, watch for the sign reading "Manitou Experimental Forest / Rocky Mountain Research Station" and turn right on County Road 79. Look to your right to see some mature beaver dams. The five mile long Hotel Gulch Road continues past the buildings and up a tight valley to the Rampart Range Road. We suggest that Hotel Gulch be driven in an all-wheel-drive vehicle and it can be quite icy in the winter.

Stop at the stone buildings to read the interpretative signage. The WPA built these buildings around 1937 and the quality and detail of the stonework is quite impressive. These Forest Service stone buildings are on the site of Dr. Bell's Manitou Park Hotels. The first hotel was built in 1874 and destroyed by fire twelve years later in 1886. He built a second hotel in 1888 that burned in 1897. After a twelve-year break, a third hotel was built in 1909 only to have it burn down in 1925. Manitou Park however, was a big success. It grew from 10,000 acres to 26,000 acres and Manitou Lake was created for the vacationing set. Cabins, tents and all the luxuries of the day could be found in this scenic valley.

In the year of William Palmer's death, Dr. Bell donated the land of Manitou Park to Colorado College that General Palmer had founded. In 1936, the Manitou Experimental Forest was established with a complex of several attractive (and nonflammable) buildings built of locally quarried sandstone. There are minimal hiking trails in this area, but it is a nice piece of local history that most drive by without knowing the story. Now you do!

Experimental Forest Research Station Stone Buildings

NORTH, SOUTH & EAST

It is true that the mountains get all the glory, but the Pikes Peak region is so much more. Until gold was discovered, the mountains were a hindrance to the progress of western expansion. The foothills and high prairie drew the first settlers.

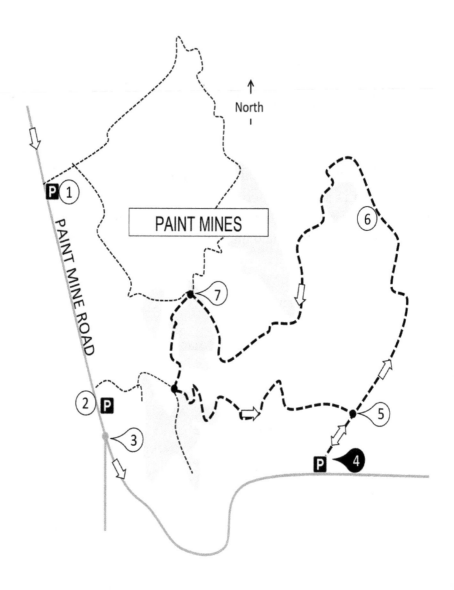

North

PAINT MINES

PAINT MINE ROAD

11
Paint Mines

The El Paso County Paint Mines
Interpretive Park
(Or "We're going to need a longer sign board")

Some day in the near future you will be sitting at home thinking to yourself that "I should be out doing something other than sitting at home." We hope that you will think of this chapter. The drive is part of the adventure here. We have always liked the transition of a drive to a destination as it gradually moves our brains into the explorer mode and away from the other side of life.

Thirty miles east of town sounds like a long way to go for a hike. If you time it right, the El Paso County Fair in Calhan in July is a perfect combination with the Paint Mines only a mile away.

Timing is everything at this park on the prairie. We are spoiled with the luxury of decomposed granite on our mountain roads and trails, but out here the clays can be a muddy mess after a rain. The winds of winter can cut through your layers of clothing on a chilly day out on the prairie. There is very little shade on a hot summer day. We prefer a clear day with a few clouds for a hike like this. This park is rarely busy, but can be quite active on summer weekends. As always in our dry climate, remember to gently hydrate. These trails are designed for hiking, so no bicycles, dogs or horses are allowed.

The free Paint Mines Interpretive Park is listed as an Archeological District in the National Register of Historic Places as well as a wildlife preservation park. Prior to being purchased by the county for preservation, these surrounding acres were primarily a grazing and agriculture area.

Long known as the Indian Paint Mines, this area has been private property and off limits to the curious until 2005. Prior to that it was just a rumored mystery and a peek through barbed wire fences to get a glimpse of the colors. On the eastern horizon, a wind farm of turbine towers can be seen. In the soil, oxidized iron, gypsum and other minerals create varied hues of clay in layers that Native American tribes have utilized for paints and pottery. Quartzite crystals add the sparkle. There is even evidence that historic and prehistoric humans have utilized the plants, animals and colorful clays of this area as long as 9,000 years ago. In the last century, these red, yellow, orange, purple and gray tinted clays were even used to create unique bricks for buildings. Artus Van Briggle experimented with these unique minerals in his pottery glazes.

Getting there: The main parking lot for the Paint Mines Interpretive Park is only one mile from Highway 24 as it passes through Calhan, Colorado. Look for the sign to the Fair

Distance: 2 mile loop
Difficulty: 🌲🌲🌲🌲🌲
Elevation Gain: minimal

Grounds. From Highway 24, turn right on Calhan Highway and go past the El Paso County Fairgrounds, then turn left on Paint Mine Road. The main parking lot **(1)** for the paint mines has good informational signage, the only public restrooms, and trail access to the larger formations. This is the most convenient location to hike into the gullies to explore the main area but we'll have you continue on. Just beyond, there is a smaller parking lot with a nice view **(2)** but poor hiking access. Keep going. As you have come to expect in this book, we are going to pass up both of these common parking lots and continue another mile.

Soon the road turns to dirt. Bear left at the perfect Y intersection **(3)** to find a third, and little used, public parking area marked only with a stone sign **(4)** that says "30550". This is your back door into the 750-acre park.

Still part of the Paint Mines Park, this hike beyond the mines will take you on a trail through prairie grasses with yucca and wildflowers, winding over a gradual rolling terrain while the wind farm is silently working away in the distance. This is the canvas behind the paint. This initial mile-long trail will intersect with the loops in the formations and main portion of the park. After the prairie hike through blue gamma and buffalo grass, you will travel through some of the colorful formations and then have the option to venture deeper in to the unique landscape or return to your starting point. There are over four miles of looping trails that all interconnect in the valleys between delicate spires, ridges and hoodoos created by eons of erosion. (See **A Step Farther** below.)

We know you want to ask. A spire is a vertical column that is wider at the base than at the top whereas a hoodoo column is thinner at the base or midsection and larger at the top. Most Hoodoos appear to have a rock balanced on top of the column. This is caused by erosion of the softer lower layers of soil in the vicinity while the hoodoo's column is protected by a harder piece or stone above and the perfect word to show up someday on Jeopardy or in a crossword puzzle.

The Hike: Review the map on the informational signage in the parking lot before your hike. From the 30550 parking lot **(4)**, follow the trail straight ahead. Soon you will pass by a junction on your left **(5)** that will be your return route from the formations, so continue straight ahead. You've heard it before; it's about the hike, not the destination. The first half of the hike will be a walk through a buffalo grass prairie, named after the bison that once swarmed this area. You may be fortunate enough to encounter pronghorn antelope, mule or whitetail deer or a prairie dog or two. If you are very lucky you may spot a coyote or a short-horned lizard. The odds are very good that you will spot a hawk or a falcon circling overhead. You may spot bits of petrified wood that should be left in place. Colorado's

124

state bird, the Lark Bunting frequents this area with a most impressive song. Feel the breeze and savor the open space.

After you pass the interpretive sign **(6)**, the trail will curve left towards the colorful formations that are best seen in direct sunlight. As you drop into the bluffs, the prairie breezes diminish and the wind farm's spinning arms disappear from sight. You are immersed in the unique landscape that is a bit too colorful to seem real, and you have yet to reach the main area of trails with the largest formations. Take off your sunglasses to see the true colors that are muted through those protective lenses and then marvel at the fact that you are the only person among the other hikers that thinks of this.

If you choose not to go deeper into the formations, keep bearing left on every major trail junction to complete the two mile loop and return to your vehicle. If you wish to continue into the formations, now is the chance to wander, but just remember this spot **(7)** to find the one mile trail back your starting point. At the lowest point of the formations you will even find some unique plant growth in the miniature wetlands.

Driving through this seemingly flat terrain between the Rocky Mountains and Kansas, the high prairie's topography can easily go underappreciated. Hopefully this ranchland stroll reminds us that geographic beauty can be found everywhere and that we should appreciate the land that we take too easily for granted.

A Step Farther:
Do You Hoodoo?

The park is quite striking and looks like it was designed by Disney Imagineers on peyote. This New Year's Day, early in the morning, I got in my first hike of the year. It's hard to believe that after living here more than 25 years, I'm still finding trails around the Front Range that I've never done before, especially gems like the Indian Paint Mines.

Want to get away from the crowds for your explorations? I was completely alone except for the occasional rabbit startled by the crunching of my boots on fresh snow. The rip in the prairie land here opens up to miles of serpentine trails featuring spectacular displays of hoodoos, caprock formations, overhangs, sculpted walls, gullies and brightly colored clay deposits. Hoodoos (besides being a really funny name) are oddly shaped pinnacles or columns of weathered rock. They create a fantastical, otherworldly landscape like something from a sci-fi or fantasy movie with colorful clay striations—bands of yellows and oranges, grays, tans, pinks and purplish mauve.

The spires and hoodoos look like solid rock, but these formations are actually quite fragile. An information brochure with map and park rules is available at the small parking lot entrance. I tried to follow all the rules. I didn't remove, destroy or disturb any of the features (I wasn't even impolite to any of them). I didn't bring in any alcoholic beverages (little early in the morning for that). I didn't discharge firearms or paintball guns, nor did I set off fireworks or explosives.

If I did break a park rule, it may have been the one about staying on the designated trails. With the snow cover, I probably strayed a bit, uncertain where the buried trail went.

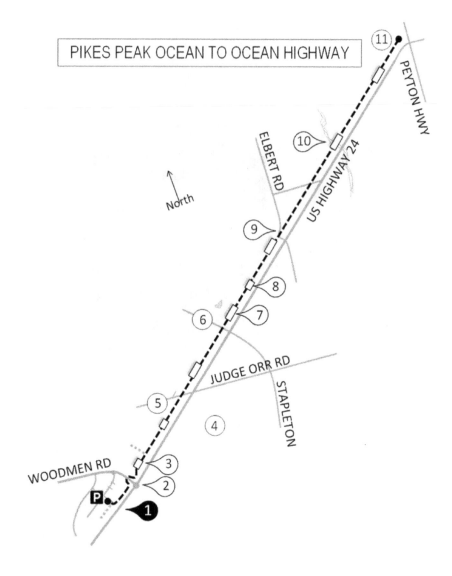

PIKES PEAK OCEAN TO OCEAN HIGHWAY

128

12

The Pikes Peak
Ocean to Ocean Highway

The highway that can't make up its mind

This exploration isn't for the mountain hiking soul. This is a flatland bike ride through flat terrain. We visit the view that the first "Pikes Peak or Bust" pioneer arrivals welcomed with celebration and relief. There was discussion that this chapter shouldn't be in a hiking book, but the story of the road's history was so good that it won out over the fact that that this "hike" is really better as a "bike."

The 1869 transcontinental railroad was the only way to get from coast to coast without a wagon and horse. It took 43 years before the idea to connect rural roads into one long coast-to-coast route came to be. Cities, counties and states collaborated to connect their dirt roads and no federal origination or funds were involved.

Distance: 20 Miles RT
Difficulty: 🌲🌲🌲🌲🌲

The Lincoln Highway was the first road to connect the nation from coast to coast, completed in 1912. Of course the definition of "highway" was much different than it is today, as the road from coast to coast was gravel at best, and muddy ruts at its worst. You may have passed the huge bust of Abraham

Lincoln on Interstate 80 west of Cheyenne, Wyoming that celebrates this historic route.

Colorado wanted to get in on the new automobile tourists traveling the Lincoln Highway because it had ignored the entire state of Colorado by rudely running through Wyoming. Other states outside of the original route felt the same, so two years later, the new 1914 route through Colorado offered direct competition with the 1912 road. Just like the Lincoln Highway, the Pikes Peak Ocean to Ocean Highway was pieced together to connect the east and west coast from New York to San Francisco. Technically, it also ran the other direction from Los Angeles to New York, but in this exciting time of westward expansion, who would want to do that? West to east was not promoted.

The Ocean to Ocean Highway had Pikes Peak in the name to show how much better this muddy route was over the other muddy route. Signs were placed at towns and intersections all across the United States from New York City to San Francisco, California.

A "PP-OO" signpost meant that you were on the right track; the message was sometimes on boards and often painted on large rocks. Promotions and bragging rights by the towns along the way were similar to that of the Route 66 phenomenon that would come decades later.

Other parts of Colorado wanted in on the tourist action, so a second route was created through this state. The western terminus later changed from San Francisco to Los Angeles. The nickname, "the highway that can't make up its mind," was given to the Ocean to Ocean Highway by the early 1920s.

In 1926, Highway 50 took over as the popular coast-to-coast route. The following year, Route 66 got all the glory, running from Chicago to LA. The PPOO Highway was later given the numerical designation as Highway 24 through Colorado.

Let's talk about your visit to a ten mile section of the route, starting in the town of Falcon. This straight-as-an-arrow trail is slightly downhill as it heads east away from the mountains, and you won't really notice it until you turn around in Peyton and find that it's a bit more work going back. It is an easily accessible exploration and we suggest using a bicycle if you wish to do the full 10 miles each way. It can be a long trip without any shade, but it is within reason for a motivated novice bicyclist to explore the entire length.

Getting there: From Colorado Springs, take Platte Avenue, Highway 24, east to the town of Falcon, Colorado. Turn left at Woodmen Road and then the first left onto McLaughlin Road. Next, take the third left at the Rock Island Trailhead sign. Picnic tables and a restroom are available. You may also take Woodmen Road east from Colorado Springs to this same location.

The hike or bike: From the trailhead parking lot **(1)**, go left on the trail heading east. (The trail to the west is a dead end.) Cross under Woodmen Road **(2)** and you are on your way, crossing over the first of many railroad bridges **(3)**. There are mile markers placed along this ten mile trail thanks to a well-executed Boy Scout project that marks your progress in both directions, as well as a few benches.

You may be fortunate enough to experience a small airplane flying low overhead accessing the Meadowlake Airport **(4)** on the other side of the highway.

As you enjoy the shaded trail through of a rare cluster trees, use caution. You exit the trees immediately at the crossing **(5)** of Judge Orr Road. You are not easily visible to the drivers that are in a hurry to get onto Highway 24. Be careful! The next crossing at Stapleton Road **(6)** isn't nearly as scary.

At the longer bridge **(7)** after Stapleton Road is a picturesque view of a small pond **(8)** and a well-worn loafing shed. An assortment of early automobiles was used to shore up the stream banks underneath the railroad bridges in this area.

At Elbert Road **(9)**, again, use caution. It is wider, with turn lanes. Your trail crossing is not the driver's priority, but your visibility is much better than the Judge Orr Road crossing.

The Green Bridge **(10)** was a landmark on the NY to LA highway. The official name of the bridge is the Black Squirrel Creek Bridge, but it was known to all as The Green Bridge. Near Peyton, at milepost 327, Highway 24 crosses over Black Squirrel Creek. The unique bridge that spanned this creek has a story. The original bridge over Black Squirrel Creek was one of the final hurdles to the trans-continental roadway.

An advanced designed Black Squirrel Creek Bridge replaced it in 1935, but this was after the original PPOO had faded in popularity. It was an iron bridge with concrete abutments. Barred windows in the abutments were rumored to have been a jail for holding transferred prisoners. Another rumor held that it was for a German POW chain gang during WWII. These memories are still active among the families that

The Black Sqluirrel Creek Bridge
Colorado Department of Transportation Photo

grew up in the area. Actually these barred entrances were access openings to remove the concrete forms during the construction of the bridge and the bars were there to keep the kids out, not prisoners in, but that story is not nearly as much fun.

The Green Bridge was on the national register of historic bridges, but it had deteriorated to the point that it had to be replaced. The Green Bridge was in such bad condition that the state couldn't give it away to be displayed at another location. The unique steel work and the mysterious window are now just memories of the people that grew up in the Peyton area. In 2011 the Green Bridge was demolished.

Junked automobiles were used as a cheap and convenient landfill along the drainages of the area and it is fun to stop at

A Willys Carryall Wagon supports the riverbank

each creek that this old railroad bed crosses. Nice assortments of antique autos are peeking back at you through the prairie grasses. An interpretive sign about the Green Bridge at Black Squirrel Creek can also be found on this hiking/biking trail.

One mile after crossing Black Squirrel Creek, you reach Peyton **(11)** and the end of the developed trail and time to turn around.

The melancholy view in this photo says so much about this historic route. In the foreground is the long abandoned concrete

The Ocean to Ocean Highway paralleling
The Chicago and Rock Island Railroad

bridge for the Ocean to Ocean Highway that ended in New York. Running parallel to the road are the remains of the wooden railroad bridge that terminated in Chicago. These historic bridges are easily seen from Highway 24 east of Calhan.

A fun finale to this chapter: I was researching an area outside of Salida, Colorado. (OK, I was searching for Forrest Finn's treasure.) As I got back in to my Jeep, an older couple flagged me down. They were volunteering at the Western Fremont History Society and invited me in. I immediately spotted a wooden sign that was leaning against the back wall. It had very recently been found lying in a field near the road. Inside the repurposed wooden church in Howard, Colorado was a "PIKES PEAK Coast to Coast HIGHWAY" sign. What are the odds that it was something I even knew about and that they took the time to flag me down? Although the wood was quite weathered, it didn't appear to be over 100 years old and I didn't find the "Coast to Coast" phrase ever being used instead of the "Ocean to Ocean" phrase. Still, what a fascinating coincidence!

An old sign recently discovered east of Salida,
but the route was never officially called Coast to Coast

A Step Farther
Eastonville Cemetery

It's close to Colorado Springs, but Eastonville Cemetery seems like worlds and ages away when you view the time periods on some of the grave stones. Many births and deaths etched into stone date back to the late 1800s, the pioneer days of the Pikes Peak Region.

Located on the prairie edge of Black Forest, the east part of this cemetery is out in the open; the west side is shaded by pine trees, where most of the markers are. In this scenic, natural setting, the ground is carpeted with pine needles and cones, wildflowers and regional buffalo grass. The entrance archway announces that the cemetery was established in 1885, but the earliest marked burial, that of baby Willie Musser, is dated 1886.

The visit here is both interesting and somber. Names on the tombstones and brief messages from by-gone days speak of lives well lived, or of those barely lived at all, cut too short to leave any legacy. On some stones, the name has been erased away completely from memory by time and the elements.

For the most part, we can get just a glimpse of a life from a wooden or stone marker: Loving Husband, Faithful Wife. Father, Mother, Son, Daughter, Baby. Uncle, Friend, War Vet.

From included etched graphics, one is an avid fisherman, another a truck driver. A carpenter, gardener, teacher, skier. Many, if not most, deeply religious, leaving behind an expression of their faith and hope with a favorite Bible verse.

So little of a life story can be captured from the space limitations of an etched marker. Just hints on a two-foot by three-foot stone cannot begin to tell the full tales of love, laughter, loss, accomplishments, adventures, sacrifice, hurt, overcoming, belonging, values, and what was really important in life for the person whose name rests on the marker. One etched message reads: "BE A LIFE LONG LIVED OR SHORT, ITS COMPLETENESS DEPENDS ON WHAT IT WAS LIVED FOR."

It's been said that there is no luggage rack on a hearse (old joke). None of us is getting outta here alive, and we are taking nothing with us. Visiting Eastonville Cemetery did give me pause for reflection as I walked up and down the rows of grave sites, most from the early days of Colorado settlement, a few still a fresh mound of earth. I felt I honored those who have passed by reading the name and message on the headstones.

Some read little more than a moniker with birth and death dates. Some told more of a story. Some markers were so weathered it was difficult to read much at all. Walking through graveyards may not be for everybody. But for those interested in regional history, and wanting to get a brief look into the lives of those who arrived before us, this is an ideal stop.

From Falcon, go north five miles on Meridian Road.

The Eastonville Cemetery is tucked away near the northeast corner of Meridian Road and Latigo Boulevard.

138

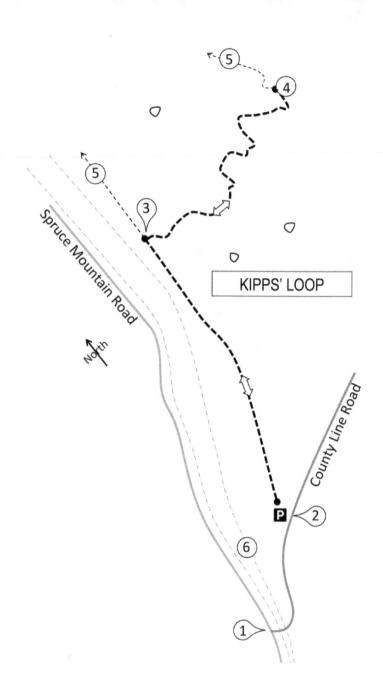

KIPPS' LOOP

North

Spruce Mountain Road

County Line Road

13
The Trails of Palmer Lake
With a visit to Mr. Kipps

Between Colorado Springs and Denver lies the Palmer Divide, an elevated ridge that creates a subtle pass between these two large cities. This ridge is better known to commuters as Monument Hill. The pass becomes more noticeable during the snow storms that are captured here and rerouted due to this ridge. This ridge splits the drainage from the nearby mountains. On the north side of Monument Hill the water runs to the Platte River through Nebraska to the Missouri River. On the south side of the hill, the water drains into Monument Creek, then on to the Arkansas River, It is amazing to think that these waters split on Palmer Divide, spill into the Mississippi River hundreds of miles apart to rejoin in St. Louis, and finally pass through New Orleans into the Gulf of Mexico.

At the base of the mountains, at the top of this little ridge, is the pleasing town of Palmer Lake. Even though the inevitable growth of newer homes surrounds the lake and original town, the speed trap curve of older buildings that is downtown Palmer Lake is alive and well.

Before Interstate 25, the original north/south highway ran through the towns of Monument and Palmer Lake, then on to Larkspur and Denver. We still drive this two lane road once in a while for a leisurely and scenic escape from I-25. It is easy to see why this route became the preferred method 100 years ago, connecting the small communities at the base of the foothills of the Colorado Rocky Mountains.

The lake came first. Palmer Lake was officially recognized in the 1830s and this natural spring fed lake was the draw for

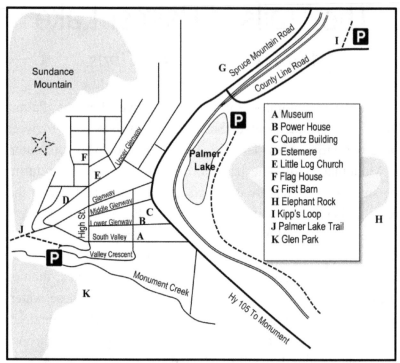

the first settlers of the area. A lone barn remains from the first homestead **(G)** in the 1860s and may still be seen in use over 150 years later. Cattle were driven between Texas and Wyoming on the famous Goodnight-Loving trail that ran nearby and the McShane Fort was near the railroad tracks east of town. Potato farming was a big deal and a yearly Potato Festival livened up the harvest season. The Palmer Lake potatoes made a good showing at the Potato Exposition every year at the Denver Western Stock Show.

In 1871, the D&RG railroad was built over this ridge, originating in Denver, heading south for Mexico and routed by this tiny lake to provide year-round water for the steam engines. After their laborious ascent of Monument Hill, the lake replenished the water the steam engines needed for the crossing. Not long afterwards, a competing railroad company built their line paralleling the first set of tracks. These two lines ran on opposite sides of the lake with similar stations on opposite shores. A large ice house was on the south shore of Palmer Lake where blocks of lake ice were harvested up until 1941 for chilling the "refrigerated" railroad cars. A number of years ago, the natural spring supply was damaged during an attempted dredging of the lake so Palmer Lake is now being fed by two reservoirs just above town that were originally created by the railroad to sustain the supply. No longer needed as a water source for the steam engine's boilers and the iced refrigerated railcars, the lake is the pride of the town and a scenic fishing and recreation spot. During drought years when the lake is dry, tongue-in-cheek residents have been heard to call their town "Palmer Meadows."

One set of the tracks through town are long gone, but the other set is quite busy. Much of the traffic is made up of coal trains from Wyoming's Powder River Basin headed to the power plants in the south and the freighter docks of the Gulf of Mexico. Just north of the lake and across the county road is a staging area **(6)** for the helper engines that would push the heavy trains over Monument Hill. Usually working in pairs, these engines would provide the extra power to make the climb and then return on the second set of tracks, ready to push again. This practice has been phased out as these heavy trains now have dedicated pushing engines on the rear.

What do Bruce Willis, Tom Hanks, Napoleon Bonaparte and astronaut Scott Carpenter have in common? Palmer Lake, of course! Scott Carpenter spent memorable summers at his grandmother's home in Palmer Lake. The Countess Katrina Murat sewed the first Colorado State Flag at her home **(F)** in Palmer Lake. She obtained her Countess title as a result of a marriage to the grandnephew of Napoleon Bonaparte. Her grave marker in Denver proudly calls her "The Betsy Ross of the Colorado Territory." And finally, pioneer Bruce Willis owned the café near Thomas Hanks' livery stable in the early 1900s. Please forgive that we could not resist such a coincidence.

The single room old town jail sits in the tiny tree shaded city park behind the local library, museum **(A)** and city offices. A few blocks away is **(E)** The Little Log Church, which is the perfect name for this slice of Americana. Two early log homes and the bell tower from the first schoolhouse were combined to create this historic building.

A wealthy dental surgeon from Baltimore had visions of Palmer Lake becoming a popular tourist destination. In 1887 Dr. Thompson built his mansion **(D)** called Estemere in the Victorian style above the town. Still the pride of Palmer Lake, this private home has eighteen rooms, a carriage house, chapel and various out buildings. Palmer Lake did indeed become a tourist destination providing a cooler wildflower and picnic outing when it became too warm in Denver or Colorado Springs—all for the price of a $1.50 round-trip train ticket.

The area called Glen Park, or The Glen, is in the subtle valley **(K)** on the southern edge of Palmer Lake and has more than its share of the town's legacy. Using this lush area, the large educational and entertaining Rocky Mountain Chautauqua (an event that became a college of the people, attracting those seeking to discuss popular issues) ran for over 20 years in Palmer Lake, ending in 1910. Colorado's state flower, the Columbine, was "discovered" by the Long Expedition in 1820 on this hillside. The prominent Rockland Hotel was also situated here, along with a petting zoo where guests could hand feed deer and a gazebo that served as a bandstand. All of this is long gone, but the gazebo still exists at its new location high on the rock wall in front of Estemere.

Sundance Mountain is the triangular backdrop to the town. In 1934, residents of Palmer Lake came up with the idea of a large lighted star above town. Erected by fire department volunteers, the flat face of this hillside holds a star that is lit for the month of December (see **A Step Farther** below). The posts that support the strings of lights were old city water pipes. These heavy pipes were carried up the mountain by sheer manpower as well as the cement, cables and other supplies used for construction. No roads or visible trails mar the face Sundance Mountain. Recently rebuilt with new wiring and LED lights, this star will continue to give Interstate 25 travelers the warm-fuzzies for many Christmases to come. Well done, Palmer Lake.

The Quartz House **(C)** is easily spotted on the west side of the road as you pass through town. It was built as a café on the Colorado Springs to Denver highway in the 1920s. The milky quartz used in construction had been rolled down Sundance

Mountain by family members. One block behind the quartz house is a square home **(B)** built of native stone. This little structure was the first electric power house for the town.

That was quite a bit of history on Palmer Lake, but we're here to talk hiking!

Getting There: From Interstate 25, take exit 161 for Highway 105. Turn left at the light and then take the first right after crossing over I-25. Follow Hwy 105 for 4 miles to the town of Palmer Lake. Watch your speedometer as speed limits vary on Hwy 105. If you are coming from the north, the County Line Road exit will also bring you here.

The Hike: To get to the Kipps Loop parking lot and the Greenland Open Space trailhead, cross the railroad tracks **(1)** north of the lake. Continue on County Line Road for one half mile to the archway **(2)** over the trailhead on your left at the bend in the road. Most of this hike is in open grassy fields and gently rolling hills with little shade. Kipps Loop is a simple 4 mile out-and-back round trip, but can become much more as it is part of the larger 8.5-mile long Greenland Loop. From the parking lot, hike one mile. Turn right **(3)** on Kipps Loop. Continue one more mile gently uphill, to find **(4)** Mr. Kipps.

Kipps Loop is named after Edward Thomas Kipps, whose solitary headstone sits just off trail, elevated in the pine trees at the bottom of a small bluff. The base of the monument states that he was from London, England. It is an impressive headstone that seems out of place on the hillside; an antique wrought iron fence completes the picture. This local cemetery was relocated long ago because it was too far from town, but we can only speculate as to why Mr. Kipps and his monumental headstone were not invited along.

This hike isn't just about visiting Kipps but more about the experiences along the way. Sights include an old stock pen, a cattle water pond, the view of Spruce Mountain to the north and the sights and sounds of an occasional train **(6)** working hard to make it over the Palmer Divide. When you are ready, retrace your steps to the trailhead.

We only focused on this hike because it has a historical element at the end, but there are several other excellent hiking options accessible from Palmer Lake. From this point you can see Spruce Mountain Open Space to the north. We recommend this hike for your to-do list. Spruce Mountain cannot be accessed from this trail but it is a quick drive up South Spruce Mountain Road.

Mr Kipps' monument

From Mr. Kipps' knoll the trail continues on the much longer Greenland Loop **(5)**. The Greenland area at the north end of this loop was named by Helen Hunt Jackson, Colorado's noted novelist of long ago. Greenland, a town that no longer exists with the exception of a few farms, won her over with its abundant grassland and picturesque bluffs. The north end of the loop can be accessed at interstate exit 167.

147

For a more challenging hike, with trees, you may want to visit the **Palmer Lake Trail.** On the west side of town is a genuine Rocky Mountain hike up a steep canyon **(J)** that will lead you quickly to the two city reservoirs and beyond. The first one you reach has been appropriately named Lower Reservoir. Soon after that the trail reaches Upper Reservoir, which is above the Lower Reservoir, apparently named because the Lower Reservoir is lower than the Upper Reservoir. Got that? At the west end of the Lower Reservoir, to the right, is the unmarked Ice Cave Creek Trail that loops around to the Upper Reservoir. The trail that extends a little beyond the Upper Reservoir leads into a nice treed valley, but no particular destination. An excellent parking area is available at the south end of High Street on Old Carriage Road.

New Santa Fe Regional Trail: Park on the east side of the lake. The Santa Fe Trail is a comfortably level route on the abandoned Atchison, Topeka and Santa Fe Railroad. This trail runs south through the United States Air Force Academy as a part of the Colorado Front Range Trail. There is also a nice walking trail around the lake.

The Colorado Front Range Trail: The Greenland Trail and the Santa Fe Trail mentioned above are part of the much larger Colorado Front Range Trail. The Front Range Trail is a long-term project to create a multi-use trail from Wyoming to New Mexico and has a trailhead access in the parking lot at Palmer Lake. This border-to-border Front Range Trail is currently about 30% complete, but the segment through Palmer Lake is a wonderfully completed 40 mile trail between Greenland and the town of Fountain. The north end can be accessed from the Greenland Exit no. 167 on Interstate 25. The southern terminus is at the ponds of the Fountain Creek

148

Regional Park near exit no. 132. Mostly hard packed dirt and minimal hills, this trail is ideal for a lengthy bicycle ride. With an elevation loss of 1,300 feet over 40 miles, it is a gradual, almost imperceptible downhill grade southbound, but you can feel the subtle climb going north.

All that and we haven't even mentioned Mt. Herman Loop and Raspberry Trail. We all know that life is what happens while you are planning life. We propose that hikes happen while planning a hike. Do you need a destination, or do you wander?

Palmer Lake is just one of many countless historic towns in Colorado, each with their own distinct personality, scenery and history. This town's four different types of trails and the proximity to the interstate highway make it especially appealing. The restaurants that have been around for ages, the curve in the road that runs through the center town, the trails and of course the lake itself will provide incentive to return when you can.

A Step Farther:
Dizzy, the light bulb-carrying dog

I stood there in wonder! Amazing! Dizzy must have been something to see! Standing nearly five feet tall—twice the size of a normal German Shepherd dog—weighing 300 pounds, and made of bronze, no less. Oh, wait … this was just a representative statue commemorating the real canine. My bad.

When exploring with Rocky around the Village Green Park surrounding the Lucretia Valle Library and Museum, we happened upon the sculpture commissioned by the Palmer Lake Historical Society for the 50th anniversary of the town's Star of Bethlehem on the side of the mountain. Dizzy represents the volunteer spirit of those who built the star … and how to exploit cheap work out of our furry friends. This was in the days before Canine Labor Laws.

Bert Sloan and B.E. Jack had convinced the men and women of Palmer Lake to construct the star on the side of the mountain above town. Of the many hard workers, one of special note was Bert's dog, Dizzy, named after the famous pro baseball player of the era, Dizzy Dean. The Shepherd was Bert's constant companion—might as well put him to work too. I hope he was rewarded at least with yummy doggy treats. Dizzy, not Bert.

Bert made a small pack that he carefully strapped to Dizzy. As the crews worked on the mountainside, Dizzy carried supplies from one group to another. A call of his name or a whistle, and Ol' Diz would come running packed with tools, nails, electrical wire, and even light bulbs. The volunteers must have learned quickly not to put the light bulbs in the same pack pockets as the hammers.

In 2013, the Star of Palmer Lake was designated as a Colorado Historic Site by the state. The lit star that greets drivers on I-25 at Christmas time as they pass up and over the Palmer Divide still shines bright to this day. Bert and Dizzy would be proud.

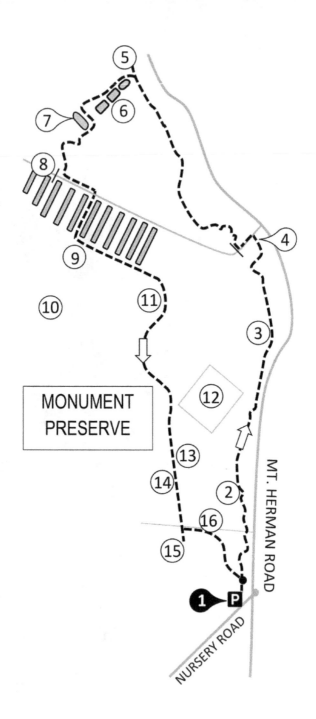

MONUMENT
PRESERVE

MT. HERMAN ROAD

NURSERY ROAD

14

The Monument Preserve

Those fascinating tree rows

This loop may be done by mountain bike, but we suggest it be done as a walk as there are many stops along the way to discover small clues to the past activities that have occurred in this grassy valley. No public restrooms are available.

In the Monument Preserve you will find the remnants of a pine tree nursery gone wild after being abandoned on very short notice. The rows of baby trees that should have been harvested were left to grow on their own leaving an unnatural alignment of matching trees sixty feet high.

This is evidence of a massive operation designed to restore our over-harvested and fire ravaged mountains from a century ago. As long as there have been mountains there have been fires. Lightning is the most common cause of our forest fires both in ancient and modern times.

Distance: 3.5 Mile Loop
Difficulty: 🌲🌲🌲🌲🌲
Minimal Elevation Gain

I once was invited into a spelunking adventure into a private cave, elsewhere in Colorado. One of the things that stuck with me the most were the pieces of charred wood imbedded into the walls of the cave that our guide stated were from an ancient forest fire ages ago.

The first documented fire in the region was in the fall of 1854, a few years prior to the white man's permanent settlement of the area. One of the largest wildfires on modern record, it was caused by man. As winter approached, the Ute Indians would move down from the mountains in search of game. Near the location of present day Fort Carson a group of plains Indians, either the Cheyenne or Arapahoe, had set a grass fire to herd the game away from the foothills and the competing tribe. Unfortunately this is when high winds kicked up and immediately drove the fire up the side of Cheyenne Mountain, over the foothills to Ute Pass. It burned where Manitou Springs is now and continued up through what would one day be Woodland Park and continued burning west. Three weeks later it reached the Monarch Pass area and finally stopped when it ran out of fuel as it reached the treeless South Park, seventy miles from the fires origin.

The healthy growing environment on the south slope of Pikes Peak had its share of massive fires a few decades later in the late 1800s. The nearby forests were harvested for lumber. Logging companies didn't have the long term reforestation concerns that we have today and lumber mills were built throughout the area supplying the demand for buildings and mines.

Recognizing that it could not continue at this pace, the federal government would attempt reforestation of the damaged and barren hills.

The idea was to create a planting station in the environs that would be similar to the mountainsides that needed the trees.

Initially a tree nursery was attempted not far from St. Peters Dome on the Gold Camp Road, but the seedlings failed to mature due to the climate and water demands. Another nursery was attempted in Jones Park above North Cheyenne Canyon, but it also failed for similar reasons.

In 1903 a quest was begun to locate the ideal area to produce the millions of trees needed for this grand challenge of reforesting the mountainsides. A large open area near the base of Mount Herman turned out to be just what they were looking for and the 7,000-foot elevation was right for the trees that

Rows of young pine trees were left to grow on their own

would be produced. A sufficient supply of water was available from springs in the area. The soil was right and a rail line was not too far away for transporting the young trees to other areas of the state. Nearby Mount Herman had recently experienced a large fire.

By 1907, the Bureau of Forests had created the Mt. Herman Planting Station as a pine tree nursery with a system that produced pine trees by the millions. Seeds were collected from pine cones to start the process. After two years the seedlings were able to handle the move into planting beds for two more years of growth. The activity during the height of the operation was a mind boggling five million trees per year shipped out and planted in the Pikes Peak Region. After the great recession, the Civilian Conservation Corps, better known as the CCC, was created to provide government sponsored work related to the natural resources of the nation. Nicknamed The Tree Army, the CCC provided a wealth of manpower for this huge undertaking and hot lunches were delivered to the crews daily. When World War II broke out, these strong workers were conscripted into the military services and the CCC very quickly ceased to exist and the seedlings in neat rows were left to grow.

Getting There: From Interstate 25 take exit 161, Highway 105, and head west over the freeway straight for the mountains. Stay on 2nd Street through the town of Monument until it crosses the railroad tracks. Turn left at the T intersection onto Mitchell Avenue. After ½ mile you will turn right on Mount Herman Road, but before you do, note the small Dirty Woman Creek Park on your left. There indeed was a woman that kept her kids and barnyard animals in a shack by the creek and it is told that she earned the stage coach stop the name of Dirty Woman.

Once you turn onto Mount Herman Road, watch for a photogenic ancient truck behind a decrepit barn on your left. Continue for ¾ mile and then turn left on Nursery Road. The parking lot is immediately on your right.

The Hike: From the parking lot you will see two trails going west into the forest. Start your adventure on the trail **(1)** to the right of the sign for a gradual uphill start to your day of exploration. This area is delightfully sprinkled with milky quartz and pine cones.

In about 300 yards, watch for a short path cutting off to the left leading to a pine tree **(2)** with unnatural bends and twists, called a culturally modified tree. Used for navigation and spiritual purposes, this culturally modified tree is one of many to be found in the Pikes Peak Region if you know what to look for, and now you do! A great resource is John Anderson's book, *Ute Indian Prayer Trees*. Examine the bends closely and you can see how the tree has grown around the line where it was bound with a woven yucca fiber rope that was used to create the odd shapes. Speculation is that the large scar near the bottom of the tree was for an infant cradle board that was made from this spiritual tree. These irreplaceable trees are to be respected and protected. Exactly like the windrows of pine seedlings that were left to fend for themselves, these culturally modified trees continued long after man left their mark. Take a moment to look into the distance, breathe deep and ponder.

The trail twice crosses the levee of a ditch **(3)** that was created to protect the nursery in the grassy valley below from uncontrolled drainage.

When you encounter the dirt road **(4)**, turn left on the road for a very short distance to the fence and then turn right on the trail behind the wooden fence. This road leads to the hotshots compound that you will pass later on in the hike. Walking on these winding curves that are also used by the mountain biking community briefly makes me think that I could be a mountain biker if it were only on the downhill half. It's the other half that keeps me in hiking shoes. When you reach a break in the trees you can see the dirt road ascending the face of Mount Herman ahead of you. Below that you can easily spot the tall, light colored Monument Rock that looks like a cylindrical column. Note how it changes shape as you progress along the trail.

The open valley to your left is the top of the nursery grounds. After winding 800 yards, you will spot the three ponds lined up neatly in front of Monument Rock. If you continue straight, about 100 feet past the trail to the ponds, you will encounter **(5)** an open concrete vault. You can carefully peer into the crumbled lid to see and hear spring water flowing towards the ponds. Walk back to the cutoff to the ponds.

The three rectangular reservoirs **(6)** were ingeniously engineered to use the rock as shade and a natural wind break to reduce evaporation of the valuable water from the ponds. As you walk around the ponds you will see that they sit at an elevation to naturally feed the acres of trees that were in the lush little hillside below. Between the second and third pond, see if you can spot a small wooden trough that would have trickled water between the two ponds. Continue on to explore around the base of Monument Rock **(7)**. Note: the rock formation is too delicate to be climbed—enjoy from circling the base only.

The Monument name is prevalent along this part of the state. Monument Creek runs from Monument Hill all the way to Pueblo, Colorado. Monument Hill is the dividing ridge between Colorado Springs and Denver. Monument Pass can be at times the scourge of winter commuters. Monument Valley Park (named for the creek) in downtown Colorado Springs has a special place in our hearts. Interstate 25 was initially called the Monument Valley Freeway. Was the town of Monument,

Colorado named after Monument Creek or was the creek named after the town? And now we are at Monument Rock. The question is, where is this famous monument that everyone seems to be so excited about? You are standing in its shadow. Before the days of road maps or even roads, natural landmarks were the only means available for navigation. The light color of this sedimentary monolith stood out like a beacon for miles amongst the dark greens of the forest. Arkose, a sedimentary rock, is comprised of feldspar and quartz that have eroded from the nearby mountains and compressed into this light colored sandstone that reflects light so well.

It is finally time to head for the rows of trees that you have been hearing so much about in this chapter. From the lowest point around Monument Rock locate an eroded trail that aims directly at the tall pines to your south. Do not take the trail that flows into the open valley. The trail to the trees will take you past the entrance gate **(8)** for the Monument Fire Center, home of a hot shot wildland fire crew. Turn left on the dirt road and walk a short distance while admiring the rows of trees unnaturally lined up in their full grown columns. The hike continues on the other side of the tree rows. Pass between any of the neatly lined rows of trees **(9)** to get the feel of how these tiny nursery seedlings have continued to grow unattended. Note the line of old iron irrigation pipes still rising up and down the middle of the trees. Irrigation was first done by means of an underground concrete pipeline. Watch your step as the end of each row has an open pipe big enough to step in. Years later, the iron pipe was laid down the middle with a riser in each row to supply water to the more mature trees. The grounds beneath the trees are nicely cleared and groomed by the hotshots. As you exit out the other side of the tall trees, turn left along the dirt road.

Up the hill to your right is the helicopter pad **(10)** for the hotshots. Continue following the dirt road along the valley watching for remnants of the large planting operation that existed here 80 years ago. As you head back down, generally stay to the right side of this little valley. Building foundations, well heads, and other infrastructure are hidden along the way. Look uphill to your right for a piece of a small foundation. Next to that is a pit with a large electric motor **(11)** for one of the many wells.

There is another large rectangle **(12)** nursery area that is void of trees for the most part. We won't be going that direction for this chapter but the next time you come through here, there are discoveries to be found! Piles of wire screen and planting bed frames that were custom made in their welding shop are hidden in plain sight. There are some very interesting valve arrangements and a few tall tree rows now full grown but not as groomed as the main grouping seen earlier. One of my favorite finds is ON and OFF with directional arrows etched in the concrete around a valve stem. Sorry I got sidetracked but it happens to me all the time.

As you continue down the trail notice the cattails and other plants that you typically see in a marshy area. Not your typical Colorado field. Why so wet? The secret is a dam 500 feet wide and 18 feet high. Where is it, you ask? The ingenuity of the nursery team continues to impress. Called a cutoff wall, this dam it is built underground reaching down to bedrock to keep the groundwater captive in a shallow aquifer. The water was suppled from wells, several springs, natural runoff and it even retained the water already used for irritation and ready for reuse.

Just beyond the cattails is an interesting **(13)** stone building. On your right is a root cellar **(14)**. The back wall is set into the hillside for protection from the sun and the building's heavy stone walls kept seeds harvested from pinecones ready for the next round of planting. At the top left of the door frame is an eyelette for a hook to keep the door closed; it is little things like that bring the past alive. A similar cold storage building on this preserve has no concrete floor as it was in the process of construction when WW II changed everything.

These steps have a story to tell

Another 150 yards down the trail you will find power lines running overhead. We will be turning left here, but not quite yet. Just beyond, on your right are some stone steps and a stone lined sidewalk **(15)** that leads to what must have been a nicer structure. A home? Use your imagination! Across the trail from the steps is the casing for a very old water faucet.

Return to follow the power lines to the first power pole **(16)**. Bear right at this pole to intersect a main trail. At this junction you will spot a small concrete foundation and there are several more nearby. Continue to your right though some large pine trees back to your starting point not too far ahead.

Once you return to the trailhead, did you notice the red sandstone blocks lining the parking lot? Would you guess that they are rough blocks cut from the Red Rock Canyon Quarry hiked in another chapter? These rough rectangles of quarried sandstone have been waiting for 100 years to be shaped into the components of a structure that never happened. It seems that the more we explore the more questions we have.

A Step Farther:
Take a friend

"Hey, look what I found over here!"

"Wow, I didn't even see that. Good find! And look over there...."

Even though I live just a few miles from the Monument Preserve, I had never explored this area beyond hiking to the dramatic Monument Rock, perhaps the namesake for my little home town. A gentle, scenic trail takes you to the monolith, beautifully reflected in a small spring-fed pond, where one might encounter a local resident throwing in a fishing line or a golden retriever splashing after a tossed tennis ball.

162

I had enjoyed walking the foothills here below Mt. Herman several times, through the ponderosa pine forests, breaking out into lush meadows (avoiding marshy areas) bordered by scrub oak. But I had not sauntered over to the old pine tree nursery area for any discoveries. This vast acreage includes access to the Pike National Forest Fire Center, home to the Pike Hotshots, but that area is private, so avoid trespassing.

A little bit of research really piqued my curiosity about the Preserve. Rocky and I decided to explore this rambling terrain together for historic artifacts of the former tree farm, and I'm glad we did. Not only is it fun to search for and discover the hidden past with someone else—to share the experience—but another set of eyes can certainly be very helpful.

I had hoped to find the remains of an old root cellar—which we found, much of the walls and doorframe intact—and some other buildings' stone foundations, but the more we searched around, the more we discovered. "Hey, look what I found over here" became a familiar phrase. After passing row after row of perfectly lined, 60-foot pines (leftovers from when the tree farm closed), we began to see more and more of the evidence of the community—really like a whole town—that once lived and worked here. If you are willing to take your time to do some sleuthing, you too can uncover remnants from a fascinating past that include a sophisticated irrigation system, pumping stations, ghosts of long-forgotten homes, and more. There is quite a story here.

Want to really enjoy these explorations and discover more? Take a friend!

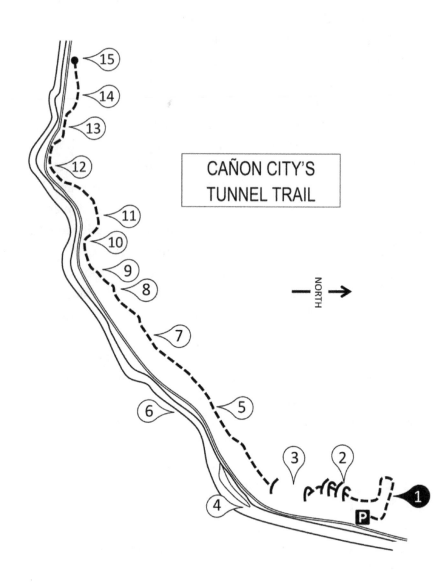

CAÑON CITY'S
TUNNEL TRAIL

NORTH →

15

Cañon City's Tunnel Trail

"It never had no rails 'cause it don't go nowhere"

Before we start, let us clear up that the squiggle over the n is called a tilde. The Spanish Ñ is pronounced "nya" when it has its squiggle overhead. Cañon is pronounced Canyon. It is said that Cañon City, Colorado, is one of only five cities in the United States with the tilde in the name, the others being in California and New Mexico. We knew you were wondering.

The Royal Gorge, outside Cañon City, is a very narrow and deep canyon at 1,250 feet high and only 30 feet wide at it most narrow point. The Arkansas River cuts through the canyon to maintain a nice steady elevation change perfect for a railroad line to get through the hills. The problem is that it is not wide enough to cut one path along the river but two lines were attempted. The Santa Fe and the D&RG railroads were competing to get to the prolific mining camp of Leadville and competition was sure to happen with that much silver waiting to be hauled out. The Colorado Railroad War was fought all the way up to the Supreme Court in 1878, and the court's judgement was for one company to build the line and the other to lease the rails. As you can imagine, this didn't last long and the war began again. Dynamite was used, granite boulders were released onto the competitor's tracks and tools were thrown into the river. Several small stone forts are still standing farther down the line, farther than we will be exploring.

Bat Masterson and Doc Holliday were there. More than just TV and novella characters, they were real people. Bat was a sheriff in Dodge City, Kansas when he was hired to protect a roundhouse in Pueblo during the conflicts and he brought in a crew including his buddy, Doc Holliday. The court's ruling attempted a compromise, but not before Bat took a civil war cannon from the memorial in front of a government building to protect the roundhouse! Both gentlemen still maintain their Colorado ties, with Bat Masterson's grave in Trinidad and Doc Holliday buried in Glenwood Springs.

Distance: 4 miles total

Difficulty:

Elevation Gain: 200 feet

The winning railroad track next to the river is now used by the Royal Gorge Route Railroad and a rock quarry. The parallel route that you will be exploring runs not far above the operating rail line. Construction ended after two tough miles. Three tunnels were blasted into the granite, two iron bridges were built and then the project was abandoned. No rails were ever laid. Today it is a level and wide gravel trail that provides a nice surface for a hike. Immediately inside the canyon, you will parallel the rushing Arkansas River and may even witness a trainload of tourists as they pass beneath you on the winner's track. No hard feelings.

Getting There: From Cañon City, head west on Highway 50 through town, also called Royal Gorge Boulevard. As you near the end of town, get in the left lane. You will see the Colorado Territorial Correctional Facility on your right. As the highway takes a quick curve to the right, watch for a left turn lane for Tunnel Drive immediately to your left as you finish the curve. Follow Tunnel Drive for one half mile to the dead end in the paved parking lot and public restrooms.

The hike is a four mile, in-and-out, round trip that can get surprisingly chilly, breezy or hot. Be prepared with light layers and water. Shade and shelter are scarce.

The Hike: As you hike the first 500 feet up an incredibly steep paved trail you will be looking for our names on the book jacket to know who to curse. You will then forgive us as the trail quickly becomes level. Halfway up this steep hill, watch for the iron foundations of an old railroad bridge **(1)** that ran above you as part of this line that never happened.

The three tunnels on this trail are at the very start of the hike. The first two short tunnels **(2)** lend themselves to some great photos when the light is right. Dynamited through the hard granite, these are typical of the tunnels found throughout the Rocky Mountains. The third tunnel **(3)** is a little longer. In contrast to the many other railroad tunnels from the early days of railroads, the ceilings are unmarred by the smoke of steam engines as the line was never completed.

Hikers tend to watch the trail for footing (a good idea) and miss the scenery above, especially when wearing a cap with a bill. So much of what we come to the mountains to see is above us. During my guided hikes I remind my hikers to look up and then illustrate that fact with the story of this spot as an example of me not following my own advice. When wildlife hears an intruder approaching on the trail the critters instinctively go uphill for defense and a predator will seek a convenient point above to watch us pass underneath. As I was exiting this tunnel a single marble sized stone bounced down from the steep cliff above. This was my startling reminder that I wasn't occasionally looking up. With a chill and an imagination running wild I instinctively swung my backpack around for access to what I may need. Directly over my head 20 feet away was the chin of a handsome big horn sheep calmly munching on a tasty branch of wildflowers. Grabbing my camera as if that was my plan all along, I took some nice photos as he watched me watch him having lunch. If he hadn't kicked that pebble loose, I would have missed out on one of my favorite hiking memories. Remember to look up as you explore.

Two of the three tunnels

Below you are two irrigation canals, one on either side of the river. Cañon City was, and still is to an extent, a farming and agricultural community. Cattle, orchards and farming were

168

successful in this banana belt of Colorado climate. These two canals were the lifeblood of the area.

On the near side of the Arkansas River you will spot the intake **(4)** for one of the irrigation canals. Convenient benches **(5)** along the way make this a civilized hike. Nearby are steel, wood and concrete clues to the past peeking out from the earth berms below the trail. The second intake **(6)** can be seen for an irrigation canal on the other side of the river. Along the uphill side of this hike the trail passes over a few dry gullies **(7)** that look like they could give a good demonstration of a "gulley washer" in action.

At the one mile mark **(8)** you are halfway to your destination. The long spindly and jointed cholla cactus can be seen all through this area. The cholla is native to northern Mexico and the Southwest United States. If your timing is right you may be lucky enough to see them sprout brightly colored flowers.

This is the first **(9)** of two sturdy iron bridges topped with timber. Underneath is a large diameter water pipeline that runs under this convenient gentle downhill grade.

There is a fourth tunnel **(10)** on this trail but this small diameter tunnel is for the water pipeline. It can be seen at trail level entering and exiting the hillside on this curve with just enough of a peek inside to drive our curiosity.

At mile marker 1.25 the ribs **(11)** of the pipeline are peeking through the middle of the trail. They were visible at the time of this publication and hopefully they are still peeking through for you to see. On the other side of the river are the remnants of a 30-inch diameter pipeline that was made of redwood with iron bands to hold it together like a very long wooden barrel. This seven-mile wooden pipeline was built in

1910 and it was surprisingly still in use until 1973! Unfortunately it can't be seen in this hike but is quite visible farther up the canyon hanging off of the canyon wall. As if we really needed another reason to want to raft and ride the rails through the canyon.

Near the 1.5 mile marker **(12)** there are large wooden power poles near the tracks. These old poles are loaded with insulators for an impressive 21 communication wires. The second sturdy bridge **(13)** is near the end of your route.

Here the trail begins to gradually descend below the line of the unfinished railroad bed. A stone wall **(14)** to your right shows what the elevation of the railroad bed would have been. Soon after this point you will see the pipeline on top of the sturdy stone walls that would have been a small drainage underpass for the railroad that never happened.

At the gated end of the trail **(15)** we can see how the canyon narrows even more and what a struggle it would have been to continue along this ledge on the cliff. By the way, the states downriver say that the Arkansas River is pronounced as the Ar-Kansas River. It is true, that is the correct way to say it but don't get me started. That's not how Colorado pronounces it. We're still working on the tilde.

The Royal Gorge Route Railroad runs parallel to the
Arkansas River, below this trestle on the Tunnel Trail

A Step Farther:
Waves on the Arkansas

I see myself as a friendly guy; for the most part, and I think others do too. I smile at strangers, feel comfortable making eye contact, and I say "hello" to most everyone I pass. In the city, this might seem inappropriate or just creepy. But in the wilderness—sharing the same experiences on trails—this is welcome and expected. Everyone does it.

On the trail systems throughout Colorado, passing hikers generally wave at each other, say "hi," "good morning," or "how are you doing?" This trail greeting ritual often leads to brief conversations to compare notes about experiences of that day, may get questions answered for first-timers on the exploration, or may simply be a way of connecting with other people (and their dogs) who enjoy the outdoors as much as I do. One may not do this on the streets of New York City without getting rebuked by a stranger, but in the wilderness, it seems quite natural to greet someone you don't know and have a bit of conversation. By talking with people, I've discovered things about the history of the trail, clarified map directions, have been sent to unexpected finds along the way, helped someone in need, learned about folk's backgrounds, something about their story, with even surprising personal disclosers. These exchanges have given me new hope about the human experience. All from a wave and a smile.

On the Tunnel Trail, an elevated level of friendly greetings will quickly be seen. As with other explorations, it's all about enjoying similar discoveries. You will still pass the occasional hiker with headphones on, plugged into their own world, one who simply nods and smiles to your "hello" and that's okay.

There are several ways to enjoy this gorge; hike it, bike it, take a train ride or an exhilarating raft trip. Take time on this exploration to not only appreciate the setting of the steep canyon walls, but also the majesty of the rushing waters of the Arkansas River—a major tributary of the Mississippi River. Popular today with rafters and kayakers, the water runs high and fast in the springtime, giving thrill-seekers a Class 5 whitewater experience under the Royal Gorge Bridge.

There are many different types of *waves* on the Arkansas. The rafters coming past you at this point may or may not return your wave as they are working hard paddling, following their guide's directions, just to survive the waves of the roaring river. They sometimes look up towards you, but rarely unless the passing train catches their attention.

Above the rafters are those riding the Royal Gorge Route Railroad. The passengers inside the cars can be seen sipping icy drinks and looking around with an occasional glance up. Those standing in the open gondola cars frequently look up the steep canyon sides and are eager to return a big wave to the hiker high above. When the first person waves, the rest peer up until they spot the colored dot on the hillside and return the gesture.

We eagerly wave at the rafters and open rail car passengers. The rail riders will wave to the hikers high above and the rafters below. That's what adventurers sharing experiences do. And waves, like smiles, are contagious.

COLORADO SPRINGS

Fortunately for us all, General William Jackson Palmer had the vision to give thousands of acres to his new town. The Colorado Springs parks system has grown along with the population and the extensive urban trails tie it all together. We don't have to go far to find the Easy Hikes and Hidden History; both may be found right under out sunburned noses.

Monument Valley Park – North Half

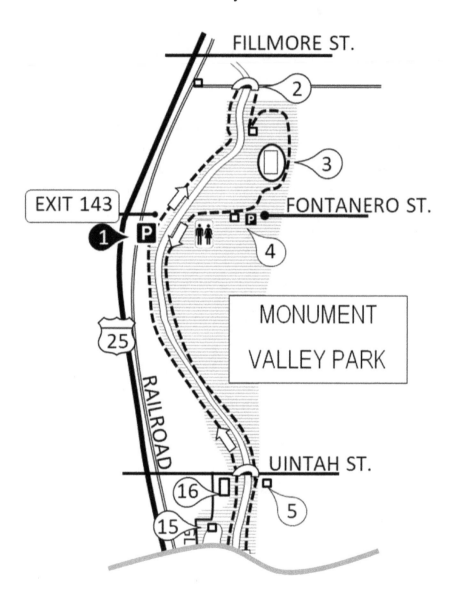

Monument Valley Park – South Half

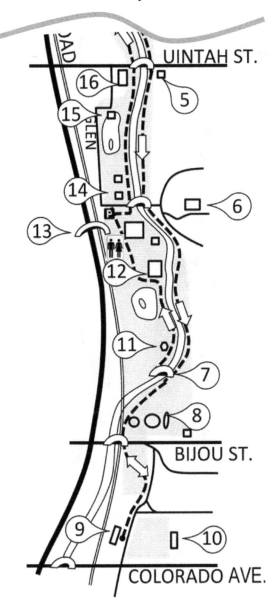

16

Monument Valley Park

A well-conceived first impression

This is an ideal exploration by bicycle due to the length. If you are walking, it is a long trek and you will have an opportunity to loop back on the bridges that cross the river to break this six mile exploration into two separate hikes. The city of Colorado Springs has PikeRide, a bike share program with electric bikes staged at the trailhead to provide the wheels if you would rather peddle the six miles.

Monument Creek begins north of town as the rivulets and ditches on the Palmer Divide combine above the towns of Palmer Lake and Monument. Monument Creek joins with Fountain Creek that flows through Manitou Springs. Fountain Creek then empties into the Arkansas River near Pueblo on its way to the Mississippi River and ultimately into the Gulf of

Distance: 6 mile loop

Difficulty:

Elevation Gain: 80 feet

Mexico. It is not a big creek but it can gain volume quickly as this little creek is the collector for the runoff from the Front Range of the Rocky Mountains in this region. Monument Creek can be a mild stream or it can be a barely constrained rushing river. It annually reflects both conditions. Snow melt and heavy rains in the foothills to the north can cause it to quickly fill from wall to wall at rare times.

When General William Palmer founded the town of Colorado Springs near the confluence of Monument Creek and Fountain Creek, the area had the geophysical attractiveness of the high prairie that we see east of town. It might as well be Kansas but with a better backdrop. (Sorry, Kansas.) He had planned Colorado Springs as a draw for the East Coast and European tourists and for investors, and he wanted a memorable first impression. Thousands of trees were brought in to create public areas and to shade his new streets and walkways. He also directed that every house in the town would have a tree planted near the curb.

All went well, but after a few decades of progress, the stretch of waterway paralleling his railroad entering the city was an unattractive entrance into town that was cluttered with creekside shacks. The newcomers were arriving by rail from a connection in Denver and Palmer needed this stretch to be filled with more trees, landscaping and small park-like structures to dress up the last couple of miles of their travels into town. He wanted it to be an oasis in the high prairie.

The park borders Monument Creek for over two miles and yet it is just a few hundred feet wide. Monument Valley Park stretches from the far northern limits of the city (at that time) all the way to the train station by his Antlers Hotel in the heart of downtown. It was an amazing gift to the city and a bit of a real estate marketing ploy that has remained a gem for the heart of Colorado Springs to this day. It didn't have to be wide, but it was long enough to parallel the tracks and give the impression of a lush city to the arriving travelers. General Palmer repurchased this land in 1903 and four years later the

165-acre park was finished. This was his strategically planned first impression.

Envision the park in a time of no freeway, no walls and fences, and very little development. (The levees that line the banks were added decades later after a destructive flood wiped out most of the park.) The railroad's tourist passengers and potential real estate customers of the day would have seen a meandering creek with the park along the banks.

This wonderful park still exists, but now the northern half is unknown to many visitors. We suggest taking the time to explore the park from one end to the other, looking for clues from the past along the way. This is a leisurely walk or bike ride with little elevation change and plenty to see along the way if you know what to look for.

Getting There: From Interstate 25, take exit number 144, Fontanero Street. Go east underneath the railroad bridge and park at the **(1)** Legacy Loop parking lot. The Legacy Loop is planned to be a 10 mile loop around the city center but only part of this adventure is on the Legacy Loop.

From the parking lot, walk north on the wide sidewalk with the creek on your right and a fenced lot on your left. You will see the park across the river. We are easily entertained by the assortment of odd city equipment behind the fence.

(2) After one half mile you will reach The Popsicle Bridge. This abandoned bridge was blocked off many years ago and left to the elements. Kids On Bikes is a group that encourages kids to get outside and provides popsicles at this turnaround point as a reward for a good ride. The kids came up with the name and it stuck. This simple and wonderful event caught on. With the cooperation of private individuals and public organizations this utilitarian crossing became so much more. It was resurfaced and painted for bicycle lanes that mimic a city street for safety lessons and benches were built to disguise a large pipe that ran along the side. We are suckers for a feel-good story and find this a touching example of how things can go right.

The Chicago and Rock Island Railroad trestle next to the Popsicle Bridge holds a line that started in Chicago and ended in Colorado Springs. This is a piece of the railroad that carried Katherine Lee Bates through the amber waves of grain in the high prairie east of town headed towards the purple mountains majesty and a summer teaching job at Colorado College. She wrote a poem in 1893 called "America the Beautiful" while she was in town, later set to music. The Rock Island Line's roundhouse and an assortment of railroad cars of the Colorado Springs Trolley Museum can be seen from here, but cannot be accessed from this location.

The well-kept Rock Island Trail parallels this railroad right-of-way east for a 6.5 mile bike ride from the Popsicle Bridge all the way to Powers Boulevard. This wide paved trail is interrupted by surprisingly few street crossings considering it spans the city from west to east. We suggest the Rock Island Trail as your adventure for another day.

To continue our exploration, cross over the Popsicle Bridge and immediately turn right onto a narrow gravel trail next to a residential wooden fence on the trail which will follow the river. Immediately after leaving the residential fences, see if you can spot the date of 7-25-38 W.P.A. etched into the concrete on top of a stone wall on the left next to the trail. The Works Progress Administration was created in 1935 by the Franklin D. Roosevelt administration to create jobs across America that would not compete with the private sector. Conveniently coinciding with the flood of 1935, unique stone work from the WPA can be spotted in various locations using native stone. Whimsical stone walls, stairs, nooks, benches and bridges will pop up along your route. After spotting a few you will quickly become a pro as recognizing their style in other parts of the park.

Once you find this etched date, retrace your steps and turn right to follow the trail next to the fences until you come to a city street. Turn right. Follow the wide trail into the park.

(3) Watch for an oval soccer field below you and the entrance to Boddington Park. Observe the raised oval that was once a dam forming the Monument Valley Park Reservoir and has now become a very creative location for this well-groomed soccer field. Boddington Park was once a reservoir along a canal system that provided irrigation water for the entire city.

Named after the kindly Mr. Boddington who enjoyed watching soccer games in the nearby field, but he all too frequently watched and helped youngsters chase their errant soccer balls rolling towards the creek. He purchased the closed reservoir and donated it to the city for a soccer field that no wild kick could escape. It can't be easily accessed from the park side and can't be seen from many angles. The only entrance to this hidden, almost secret, sports field is from the residential street above. It still retains the lake's terrain with a steep oval ridge circling the manicured turf. Mr. Boddington's feel good story was a century before the Popsicle Bridge and is one more example of what makes this park special. I am sure that the benevolent Mr. Palmer would agree.

Continue on the widest trail around this soccer-field-in-a-bowl. Take the wider left fork of the trail until you reach a tiny stone bridge near a parking lot. **(4)** The little dry stream bed underneath the bridge leads to a waterfall wall at the geologic column and is one of the last visible pieces of the El Paso Canal. These layers of stone were collected from Queen's Canyon near General Palmer's home.

The El Paso Canal started in a collection structure at 34th Street and Colorado Avenue. (This is still in use and can be seen behind the Safeway grocery store.) The canal ended in Prospect Lake in Memorial Park. There were two lakes built along the way, the one that is now Boddington Field that you just visited and the second is now Boulder Park at North Hancock Street and Boulder Street, near Memorial Hospital and the Olympic Training Center. If you visit Boulder Park, notice the vague depression that hints that it was once a reservoir. In today's developed city it is hard to envision a connecting line from West Colorado to this little ditch and then to Memorial Hospital and on to Prospect Lake. An open canal this size was quite an undertaking but then water has always been a challenge for this semi-arid (technically, an alpine desert) village at the foot of the mountains.

(4) A must-see in the northern portion of Monument Valley Park is this almost hidden geologic wall, one of the most intriguing features in the park. A variety of stones collected from the area were artfully laid to create a wall that tells a story of the geologic layers beneath our feet. You guessed it: this was General Palmer's idea.

If you are walking, take the stone steps down beside the waterfall. If you are biking, follow the wide trail that you were

The Geologic Wall in Monument Valley Park

on and then turn right to access the geologic wall. Note that the waterfall that once used the canal now uses the runoff from city streets above. Originally, this waterfall fed a pond in the meadow below.

The Friends of Monument Valley Park (www.fmvp.net) have done an admirable job of restoring and enhancing much of the stonework in this gem of a park.

Go past the restrooms and playground to return to the trail above the river. Be careful not to follow the trail down to the river but bear left to rejoin the path on top of the levee. This is an excellent area to view what the natural hillside terrain leading to the creek looked like prior to the construction of the levees. Visually follow the slope of the land from the park, picture how it would continue below the elevated trail, and then see the slope continue below the levee into the creek. When you can visualize this, you will never look at the park the same again.

Peer down the face of the levee once in a while. The steep surface is a cobbled mismatch of broken sidewalks, sandstone slabs and large slate paving stones. It would seem logical that the WPA would have used remnants from the destruction of the flood that caused the need for the levees in the first place.

Follow the trail as it passes underneath Uintah Street and keep following the river. You are now 1.2 miles from your car. Immediately on your left, after you cross under the Uintah Street Bridge, are some tennis courts **(5)**. Behind these tennis courts is a special cluster of pine trees. This spot contains largest of only three known Lacebark Pines in Colorado, a light skinned tree with multiple trunks and a unique bark. The other two are in the Denver Botanic Gardens. An adjacent sign states that this Pinetum was created in 1909. We never knew that was a word.

A bit farther down the trail on your left is Colorado College's Washburn Field. If you are lucky you may witness a Lacrosse game or other practice sessions through the chain link fence.

The Jack Quinn's Running Club uses this trail by the river as a portion of their weekly 5k on Tuesday evenings. There frequently can be over 1,000 runners and walkers in the summer but it doesn't seem that many as they are spread out over a couple of hours. Tuesdays in the winter are understandably not as busy but a line of runner's headlamps and dogs with lights attached to their jackets liven Tuesday nights on the trail.

You will pass one of several concrete mileage markers for the Pikes Peak Greenway, and this is also part of the Front Range Trail.

The sidewalks for Queen Palmer's
Formal English Garden are still there today
Google Earth 2019

As you approach the Mesa Road crossing, look up the grassy hill to your left. On the hill above this lawn is the Colorado Springs Fine Arts Center, a wonderful art deco building **(6)** worth a long visit when you get the time. This building's location was the early home to Julie and Spencer Penrose, the founders of the Broadmoor Hotel. Cross over Mesa Road and continue to follow the creek. Across the river you can see the modern heart of the park. Don't worry, we will be returning along that side very soon. Continue on this side of the river to stroll past stylish homes of the era, modern condos and some more of the fanciful stonework.

Soon you will reach a footbridge **(7)** that crosses the creek. It's time to make a decision. Straight ahead is an optional spur for your trek through the least attractive section of today's adventure, but will quickly pop you out at the historic D&RG railroad depot and the Antler Park.

To get the full story of the traveler's final approach into the city, this end of the park should be seen. This spur is a quick 1/3 mile long and you will be turning around to come back on the same route. If you choose to skip this spur, cross west over the footbridge to begin your return trip. Note: If you choose to continue on, do not take the paved trail that crosses under the railroad bridge, but remain on the gravel path straight ahead.

(8) After you pass by the footbridge and head towards downtown, you will immediately pass through a small circular amphitheater that once was a happening location for music and entertainment. Long forgotten, it has seen better days. Walk up the grassy embankment behind it to find large oval sidewalks. Above these ovals are more decorative walkways. William Palmer and his wife, Queen Palmer, were fond of English formal gardens and they had created this area to showcase this style. Queen's gardens were restored in the 1990s but were not maintained by the city. Now just lawn and sidewalks, envision this oval and the land around it trimmed with symmetrically groomed hedges, flowerbeds and garden paths.

The anticipation of the arriving passengers must have been great as their train slowed down approaching the depot. Looking south from here, note the Monument Valley Park's iron archway on Bijou Street that once proudly faced the city center. This main entrance from the past has all but been lost as the modern Bijou Street commuters zip past on their quest for the I-25 onramp. It is getting a bit citified at this point, but there are more things to discover in this MVP of a park. (Get it, MVP?)

(9) Continue your walk through the unattractive trackside underpass beneath Bijou Street Bridge and on to the small street. Bear right on the sidewalk and head for the stone Victorian style D&RG Railroad Depot. Peek in the windows to see the original walls of the old depot. Just for fun, see if you can find, on the north end of the railroad depot, a 1922 brass commemorative plaque that is being lifted up by the overgrown roots of the very tree that it is commemorating.

(10) The railroad depot is facing the Antlers Park and beyond that the Antlers Hotel. The early Antlers Hotel faced the park with a grand façade and welcoming stairs and patios. You can visualize the Antlers Park as a grand entrance to the city as they disembarked from the train. Landscaped walkways led from the depot directly to the hotel. It was the perfect place to stretch your legs after a long train ride and admire this Little London in the west. The first Antlers Hotel was a wooden Victorian style building that burned down in 1898 after a fire at the railroad freight depot three blocks away reached the hotel. The fire overtook boxcars loaded with explosives destined for the mines of Cripple Creek. The flaming debris from the blast and the high winds set the three nearby lumber yards ablaze and easily spread to the wooden Antlers Hotel.

The second incarnation of the Antlers Hotel was a stately stone building with a grand staircase that beckoned into Antlers Park. The ornate stone hotel was demolished in 1964 and the current cubic version took its place, turning its back on the legacy of Antlers Park.

For a moment, put yourself into early visitors' high buttoned shoes. Your train slows down as it passes the groomed park along Monument Creek. You disembark at the depot and then a walk through the shade trees and flower beds of Antlers

Early Antlers Hotel seen from Antlers Park
Detail from an antique post card

Park and up the grand staircase into the stately Antlers Hotel. At the top of the stairs, you turn around to marvel at the view of Pikes Peak rising above the train that you recently, and happily, disembarked. You just may stay in this new Colorado town. The Wild West isn't so bad after all.

From here, the restaurants of downtown Colorado Springs are temptingly close. Take a break for lunch! When you are ready, retrace your steps back under the Bijou Street Bridge and cross over the **(7)** footbridge to the other side of the creek to

189

continue your walk back to your starting point. We hope you take time to stop on the bridge and watch the water. Once you cross the bridge, turn right on the gravel path and parallel the river for your return.

(11) Not far from this bridge you will pass a stone wall next to the trail and right behind that is a short octagonal column with a bowl mounted in the top. When Colorado Springs was founded in the 1870s, the Springs part of the name was added to draw tourists and investors from the east and overseas. Borrowed from the Manitou Springs' claim to fame, there were no natural springs in Colorado Springs. That changed when this spring was tapped strategically near the river within the park's boundaries. This hexagonal stone fountain was built along with an attractive gazebo to shelter and enhance it. The townsfolk could proudly direct the queries of the newcomers to the Tahama Mineral Spring, the springs of Colorado Springs. Tahama was a Sioux Indian that assisted Lt. Zebulon Pike in his explorations in this region in the early 1800s. The gazebo over the spring was damaged along with much of the park's infrastructure in the 1935 flood and then destroyed in a 1965 flood. After that, the Tahama Spring was permanently capped. You can spot the remains of an old stone drinking fountain underneath a large shade tree a little bit farther down the trail.

Next is the small Shadow Lake with an island in the middle. When the levee was put in, the eastern half of the lake was removed. On the east side of the little lake underneath the levee, note the second level stepped down below the trail. This is the lake's dike and the trail above it is the levee that was added later across the top.

(12) After the pond you will spot the bathhouse, swimming pool and nearby pavilion that were built in 1914. Turn left in

front of the bathhouse and then right on the concrete sidewalk passing the playground and restrooms in the heart of this long skinny park. This is the busiest area that the vast majority of park users see as Monument Valley Park, but now you know there is so much more out there.

The sound wall that protects the park from the traffic noise should be on your left. On your right will be the popular Pickleball courts. **(13)** The spiraling ramp for a lengthy foot bridge over the freeway gives access to the older residential neighborhoods on the other side. We recommend taking the time to ascend this bridge that crosses over the railroad tracks and the freeway for a sensory overload created by the people in a hurry and a unique view of the activity below. Okay, that is enough of that. You will now appreciate the peace and quiet of this walk in the park even more than before. Return back down the same ramp and turn left headed towards the parking lot. Rejoin the trail next to the river and cross the street.

(14) This rock garden across the street from the parking lot was created in 1932 by a master landscaper of the time. He instructed that the boulders be left as they dropped from the truck for a natural look. Take time to walk the small loops and read the tiny signs. This is yet another unique piece of the park that so many overlook.

Continue your walk towards the scenic lake with benches under massive shade trees and the eager fowl that will suggest that you should ignore the Don't-Feed-the-Ducks sign. Don't believe them.

Red sandstone portal and lake

On the north end of the lake near the sharp bend in the road, discover two rough carved sandstone pillars **(15)**. It is obvious that this rough quarried sandstone predates the WPA stonework and is from the very early years of the park. One can picture this road as a dirt trail headed towards the lake. Were these two sandstone columns a welcoming gateway into the park in line with an old road or path alignment? Was it a trailhead entrance that leads to the long gone stream that fed the lake in the stone lined culvert nearby? Was it a signpost with the park's name? Hidden discoveries like this make us think way too hard.

Follow the road to the Horticultural Society's heritage garden. **(16)** In this garden you will discover a large representation of Van Briggle's Lorelei vase. Around the base is a circular quote "Love makes time go. Time makes love go." This ring was the border around a large clock on face of the Marksheffel garage. We give kudos to those that had the foresight to not only save it, but to hide it in plain sight to be discovered.

Just beyond this garden is the unique brick Van Briggle building on the corner of Uintah Street and Glen Avenue. Built as a pottery factory, the park side location was chosen to be an inspiration to artisans and their visitors. The chimneys of the kilns protrude from the top and an assortment of their works is inlaid in the structure to showcase their wares. It was a souvenir stop for the railroad passengers and had a showroom

Love Makes Time Go
Time Makes Love Go

of tiles that could be shipped home. After you admire the colorful Van Briggle tiles and fanciful brickwork on the exterior, join the trail to cross beneath the Uintah Street Bridge. After you cross under the bridge, there is an area that was built for access to the river. There is discussion about someday having a river walk for the city and this little river landing could be the preview of something big. Denver and Pueblo already have their comely river walks in place.

Follow the trail along the river to return to your starting point at the Legacy Loop parking lot. Hopefully the historical discoveries along the way kept it from feeling like six miles.

Today's word is Pinetum. Quite a park, eh?

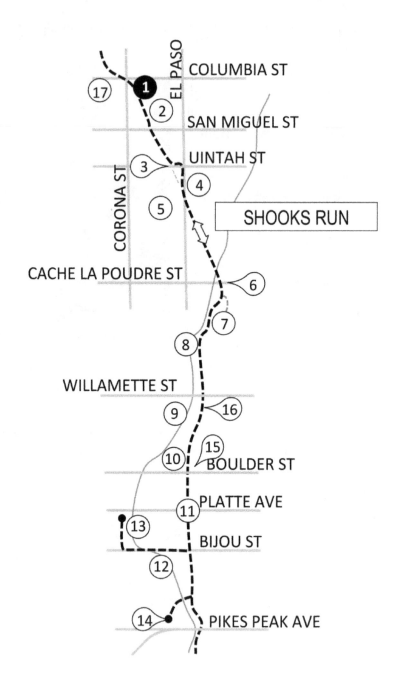

SHOOKS RUN

17

Shooks Run

The parks of a historic neighborhood

The full length of this trail is twelve miles long, running from Fillmore Street on the north to Fountain Boulevard on the south, but we are only interested in the center section for this exploration. Of course the other portions of the trail are nice too, but we are focused on the historical trailside finds and this middle part has the best variety.

The rails for the Atchison Topeka and Santa Fe railroad were pulled up in 1972, providing the city a flat path along the eastern edge of downtown and giving us the trail through the older homes of Shooks Run. The Shooks Run Trail is a major piece of the Legacy Loop. (https://coloradosprings.gov/parks/page/legacy-loop)

What is a run? Shooks Run is a stream that originates from the reservoir on the nearby Patty Jewett Golf Course, the third oldest golf course west of the Mississippi. Even if you are not a golfer, it is worth a visit to have lunch in their historic clubhouse. The name of the creek comes from the Shook brothers who owned an 80-acre cattle ranch in this area. Does it bother you that there is no apostrophe in the name Shooks Run, just like the missing apostrophe in the Pikes Peak name? Me too. Since 1890, the Board on Geographic Names has discouraged possessiveness of places by not allowing the apostrophe.

The very first platting of Colorado Springs used Monument Creek as the western boundary and this tiny Shooks Run as the eastern edge of town. Columbia Street was the northern boundary, which means that you will be starting your exploration in the northeast corner of the first plat of Colorado Springs.

Situated in an older residential neighborhood, the Shooks Run Trail has no less than three trailside cafes with outside seating to watch or be part of the activity. People-watching is an enjoyable way to spend some downtime trailside; the bigger the city the better the trailside action. After work, the first piece of business for the returning urban dweller is to walk the dog—often still in work attire as their dogs refuse to delay any longer. We suggest starting and ending your hike from the patio of the café on the southeast corner **(1)** of Columbia and Corona.

Getting There: From Interstate 25, head east on Uintah Street for one mile. Turn left on North Corona Street for two blocks and then park on North Corona Street near the intersection with East Columbia Street.

The Hike: At the intersection of Columbia Street and Corona Street it is easy to spot the trail cutting diagonally through the intersection. Nearby are a rack of electric bikes provided by the city's bike share program (www.pikeride.org). As this "hike" is more of a walk or a bike ride, this is a good opportunity to try out an *electric* bike. Not a bad idea. And fun! Hike or bike, it's a nice 3.5 mile exploration along several streamside parks. Access the trail south of the café's patio, passing a tile mosaic train engine sculpture. We'll talk about a few more of these concrete sculptures on our adventure.

As you begin, on the left you will see a complex of newer homes that share a common theme. Look for the large rectangle building with the round window close to the trail. Notice how high the garage door is. This entire block once held numerous large greenhouses for the city of Colorado Springs. When the greenhouses were removed, only the building that held the massive steam boiler was left standing, giving this modern complex a large, old and very unique storage building **(2)**.

Your second street crossing will be at a traffic light. Turn left on the sidewalk to the intersection. Uintah Street **(3)** is a busy east-west thoroughfare and although it's tempting to shortcut, wait for the signal and then follow El Paso Street for about one block. You can see where your trail cuts at an angle and you can join it again quickly. After crossing Uintah, there are some flat-roofed yellow brick buildings **(4)** with signage in an attractive font that is reminiscent of another era. These are the offices for District 11, the largest school district in the state of Colorado. The brick buildings are a mid-century style built in 1956 lending some personality to the neighborhood.

On your right is the North Middle School **(5)**. Built 1n 1926 of the same yellow brick, this school was built on the grounds that the traveling circus would pitch their tent every year. A 1920 newspaper article tells of a kite flying contest on "the old circus grounds at Corona and Yampa". That must have been fun for the kids the first few years to think they were going to their new school on the circus grounds.

Our trail first encounters the Shooks Run creek at East Cache La Poudre Street. As you cross the bridge **(6)** over Cache La Poudre Street, stop at both ends and see if you can spot where the river crosses under the road. It feels odd because the train, street and river all intersect at this exact point. The road actually dips down to cross over the river and it can be prone to flooding. Take a moment to notice the mural covered abutments for the train trestle that were built around 1918.

Just beyond the bridge you will encounter the first in a series of parks. Stay on the trail as it bears to the right **(7)**. On your right is a circular sidewalk with a unique concrete and stone bench **(8)**.

Willamette Street is your next intersection, named after the river in Oregon. Colorado residents pronounce it Will-uh-MET. This drives the people from the Pacific Northwest crazy. Try it on a Northwestern friend. The correct pronunciation is wy-LAM-it. Colorado Springs' downtown main streets are named after landmarks that General Palmer encountered in his explorations. Names for the east/west roads downtown are named after rivers and the north/south streets are named after mountain ranges.

Just after you cross Willamette (reading this, did you pronounce it correctly), look to your right for a large mural **(9)** on the retaining wall of the river painted by neighborhood volunteers through the prolific nonprofit, Concrete Couch (www.concretecouch.org). The mural on the Cache La Poudre train abutments, the mosaic train and the concrete art bench are also part of their work. As you get to recognize their work you will spot more and more of this nonprofit's contributions all over town. A bit farther down the trail, tennis and Pickleball courts are trailside.

As you approach the Boulder Street intersection, a community garden **(10)** is on your right. Created through the Pikes Peak Urban Gardens (www.ppugardens.com), you find these in several locations around town including some public school grounds.

At the Boulder Street crossing there is a crossing signal **(10)** just for you. Crossings for trails should all be this responsive because we can be an impatient lot. When you press the button, a "no turns" sign immediately lights up followed by the traffic light stopping traffic and then you get your walk signal all in the first few seconds. Wow, nice.

There is very little to remind us that this was once a

The sturdy railroad bridge over Platte Avenue
supports only the weight of pedestrians today

railroad before it became an urban trail lined by parks, but the bridge over Platte Avenue **(11)** boldly reminds us. It is hard to miss this sturdy iron structure designed to hold thousands of tons as we lightly cross above the busy Platte Avenue.

At Bijou Street, turn right and go one block. On your left is the John "Prairie Dog" O'Byrne City Park **(12)**. Prairie Dog and his elk lived in this Middle Shooks Run neighborhood in the 400 block of East Bijou Street from 1903 to 1920. You will read more about Prairie Dog and his two elk, Thunder and Buttons, in **A Step Farther**, below. Turn right on North Corona Street. Frank Waters Park **(13)** may be one of the smallest parks in the Colorado Springs city park system. The City of Colorado Springs is proud to have over 9,000 acres of city parks and Frank Waters Park is a charming, tiny piece of that. Part Cheyenne, Frank Waters was an award-winning author of historical fact and fiction about the southwest. His house was close to Mr. O'Byrne's elk pen, but a few decades later. Shooks Run's stream bed is the backdrop to the little park. As you hike around this little park, note the mural of concrete on the back wall. Return back to the trail the way you came on Bijou Street and then turn right to continue down the trail.

Just before you reach the underpass below Pikes Peak Avenue, turn right on the narrow bridge **(14)** crossing over Shooks Run. This will quickly place you on a cul-de-sac that is the turnaround point for this exploration. Much can be seen from this circular dead end. Looking west is the classic view of Pikes Peak rising above the city center. Directly across the street is the historic red brick Santa Fe depot. Until the 1970s two railroad tracks ran parallel to Denver. Our trail carried the northbound trains, and the tracks that are still in operation next to Monument Creek handled the southbound trains.

The Shooks Run trail continues south for another mile and has more to see but at this time the trail loses its focus and is not the pleasant park experience we are looking for. Some day in the near future this will be the southern connection for the Legacy Loop around town but for now this cul-de-sac is a good place to turn around.

A nice surprise is preserved along the trail

On this exploration we have focused on the parks and the trail, but on the way back make an effort to notice the unique older homes built around the end of the 19th century. Retrace your route. When you get back to Boulder Street **(15)** there are two larger houses on the northeast corner called the Colorado Springs Sustainacenter. This is a project of the UCCS Sustainability Center; these offices are provided to organizations that make a positive difference in the community.

Just before crossing Willamette, notice the display of the dairy sign **(16)** painted on a gabled roof next to the road on your right. In early photos, the rectangle above the words on the sign once held a tin Coca Cola sign. Someone, at one time, made the effort to save this gable and we all benefit from this decision.

A step back in time at the Skelly Gas Station

Once you return to your starting point, we have one more treat for you. Walk across Corona Street to the Skelly Gas Station **(17)**. Overgrown by ivy and cluttered with antique Willys vehicles, this gas station still has the original signage and tons of personality. There is even a classic finned Cadillac waiting at the gas pump in this little diorama from an earlier time.

It is time to hit the patio at the café and review today's hike, but first we would be remiss if we didn't tell you that exactly one more mile north on the trail is a 1955 Tasty Freeze Drive-In with hamburgers, soft serve cones and picnic tables right on the trail. We think we may just do that extra mile.

A Step Farther:
Prairie Dog O'Byrne

If Santa Clause can pull his sleigh with reindeer, why not use elk to pull a carriage? Well, that's just what one eccentric resident did in Colorado Springs in the late 1800s.

John "Prairie Dog" O'Byrne was born in Ohio to Irish Catholic immigrant parents. His family moved toward the untamed west following the railroad, as his father was a supervisor for crews laying down track. Before arriving in Colorado, young John had witnessed scary encounters with Indians, lived through the grasshopper plague of 1874, saw gunfights, experienced Kansas tornadoes, and saw horse thieves hanged at sunrise.

Prairie Dog O'Byrne (he had a prairie dog on his carriage seat that he would pet, hence the nickname) traveled across the United States and Mexico as a railroad brakeman and arrived in Colorado Springs in the late 1800s when he was still in his 20's. He made a living as a tourist guide around Old Colorado City area, entertaining customers with dramatic stories of his past adventures. He even took visitors all the way up the dirt road to the top of Pikes Peak in a wagon drawn by four horses.

In 1888, Prairie Dog acquired two young elk in an auction in Denver. He trained them and gave them the names Thunder and Buttons. A restaurant and saloon today in Old Colorado City bears the names of those elk. In an expression of braggadocio, Prairie Dog claimed he could drive his elk-drawn carriage fast enough to make it from the gambling joints in Old Colorado City to downtown Colorado Springs in six to seven minutes. If so, it must have been a harrowing ride for the passengers, a thrilling sight for those on the street, and traumatic for the elk!

A small park bearing his name on this exploration memorializes this colorful character. A sign gives some details about the man, and you can even see a historic photo of Thunder and Buttons pulling a carriage.

Another Step Farther:
A Building's Last Stand

The Phantom Canyon Brewing Company was the first restaurant in Downtown Colorado Springs to be added to the National Register of Historic Places. It's located at 2 East Pikes Peak Avenue in the historic Cheyenne Building, a 1901 edifice that originally served as the local office for the western terminus of the Chicago Rock Island and Pacific Railroad.

During that time, the second and third stories were used for hotel rooms with shared bathrooms for the employees of the railroad system. The Cheyenne Building, however, didn't serve the railroad long. Through the years from 1909 to 1963, the building was used as a cheap hotel for tourists preferring less lavish accommodations than the Antler's Hotel across the street.

In the 1970s and again in the 1980s, the Cheyenne Building was slated for demolition to turn the corner into a parking lot. That's what we need: more parking lots, less historic buildings. Once the Historic Preservation Overlay Zone stepped in, this building may have been saved from the wrecking ball due to a stone carving of Chief Two Moons over the corner of the front entrance.

The chief participated in Custer's Last Stand and other skirmishes with the federal government in the 1870s. After the surrender of the Cheyenne band that he led, Two Moons enlisted as an Indian Scout, and due to his amiable personality, he was eventually appointed head of the Cheyenne Northern

Reservation, and even made multiple trips to Washington, D.C., to lobby for better conditions on the reservation. Two Moons was one of the models used for the design of the Buffalo nickel (minted from 1913 to 1938). Look at one of those coins again sometime and see his likeness!

This wonderful old building—now housing the Phantom Canyon Brewery—is a great visit for a step back into history, but also a fun stop for a cold one. It also boasts of having the largest billiard hall in Colorado Springs, located on the second floor.

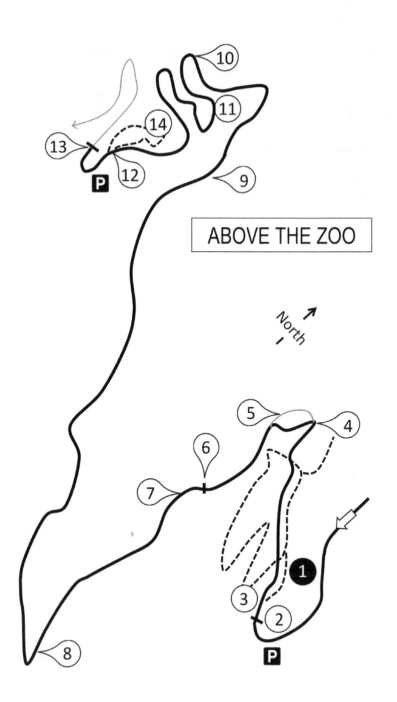

ABOVE THE ZOO

North

18

Above the Zoo

A Journey Through Hell's Gate to Sheercliff Loop

This adventure begins with as much hillside walking as you can handle, followed by a drive up a winding mountainside road and then ends with a breathtaking view from a five story tower of granite built on the side of the mountain, 2,000 feet above Colorado Springs.

Cheyenne Mountain (www.cmzoo.org) is second only to Pikes Peak as the recognizable backdrop for the city of Colorado Springs. The Cheyenne tribal legend knew this mountain as a buffalo, and the shape can be seen with some imagination. The plains Indians with a different perspective saw the mountain as a dragon. The Thirsty Dragon can be seen from the plains with the ridge of granite making up the tail on the north.

This mountain has a lot going for it in addition to the famous zoo. There are the massive blast doors that protect five acres of Cheyenne Mountain Air Station's tunnels, formerly known as NORAD. The most recognizable sight on the mountain is an antennae farm on top of the main summit that can be seen for miles. On the north side of Cheyenne Mountain is the Old Stage Road that will ultimately reach Cripple Creek by way of the Gold Camp Road. Cheyenne Mountain is a showcase of aspen colors in the fall and a year round magnet for the clouds passing through the area. There are a large number of trails in Cheyenne Mountain State Park where the Dixon Trail challenges hikers to reach a loop around the antenna farm 3,000 feet above.

1926—The new road shines in the morning sun
Detail from an antique post card

The Broadmoor Hotel was opened in 1918 where Spencer Penrose kept his collections of animals at the hotel until his monkey bit a small child. He was strongly advised that it was time to move his collection from his hotel, so the zoo was created on the mountainside in 1922. Three years later, the road to the top of the mountain was cut from the zoo to the summit, carved and blasted through the massive granite that makes up the mountain. Fresh breaks in granite expose a white and reflective collection of minerals as seen in this 1926 photo.

Now, Penrose was as popular as a man could get, but the residents of the city were not happy with their backdrop

The Cheyenne Mountain Highway
ca. 1925-1935. History Colorado. Accession #978.84

Note that the Shrine of the Sun had not yet been constructed.

sporting this new squiggle running up the face of their prized mountain. The roadbed itself wasn't as visible as was the newly exposed stone immediately above and below the cut. As you will see on the drive, a cut in a steep hillside will bare granite above the road and create the fill cascading below the road. Picture a 60-ft swath of bright and highly reflective stone in the morning light. Due to the pine tree growth and the discoloration of the granite, this cut is barely visible today.

Spencer Penrose then built the pueblo style Cheyenne Mountain Lodge, nicknamed the Honeymoon Lodge, on top of the mountain at the end of this spectacular zig-zag road. It had a restaurant, a curio shop and four hotel rooms. This was demolished in the 1970s and replaced with the Broadmoor Hotel's Cloud Camp in 2014. Today, the upper half of this tenacious road is closed to the public but the lower half is just as special and available for you to explore.

For the flatlanders out there, a switchback is created when a road needs to gain elevation in a restricted amount of space. The "W's" on the Pikes Peak Highway are a perfect example. Cheyenne Mountain's switchbacks had entertaining names when the highway first opened in 1925 with such signage as Sheercliff Loop, Hell Gate, Paradise Trail, The Spiral Shelves, Cloudland Loop, Vista Grand Swing, Multi-Vista Swing and ending at the Devil's Horns. The truth is it's a safe road with beautiful twists and turns.

The Cheyenne Mountain Zoo is consistently rated as one of the top zoos in the nation mostly due to its unique mountainside location and the active giraffe program. Above the zoo is a road full of switchbacks that you may drive with the purchase of a zoo ticket. Surprisingly, the majority of the visitors don't take advantage of the option to drive through the zoo and access this famous road up to the Shrine above.

There was a miniature cog train that connected the zoo to a lakeside depot at the Broadmoor Hotel. This little train used the same technology that made the steep Manitou and Pikes Peak Railway possible.

On display in the south end of the zoo's parking lot is the custom engine made by Cadillac **(1)** that was used to power this cog train in the 1950s. (See **A Step Farther** below.) This little white engine is sitting on a piece of the original track and the

The tunnel entrance still exists, covered in brush

tunnel underneath the road still exists. The tunnel is partially blocked but the 1957 concrete entrance can be found hidden in the brush behind the engine. A piece of the raised railroad bed parallels the entrance road just beyond the tunnel's other end.

211

Getting There: From Interstate 25, take the Lake Avenue exit number 138 and head for the mountains. At the roundabout in front of the Broadmoor Hotel, turn left to drive between the exquisitely groomed Broadmoor golf courses. At the four way stop sign, turn left following the sign to the zoo.

The Hike: The physical hiking part of this adventure is at the zoo. Park in the parking lot, purchase your admission **(2)** and walk in. Keep your receipt as it will be your ticket to venture beyond the attraction.

Wander the zoo and explore. There is no wrong direction, but there is more than enough elevation ups and downs to give you a workout. Feed the giraffes by hand and visit the new Waters Edge building. Let the budgies land on you as you feed them in the Australian Walkabout.

You can see the Will Rogers Shrine of the Sun beckoning to you from a granite perch above. The chimes from the tower remind you that there is more adventure ahead. This hillside zoo will burn the calories and entertain at the same time. Admire the organization's education and conservation efforts. When you are ready for the next part of your adventure, return to your car and drive to the main gate. Really, you can drive right through the middle of the zoo! Be on the alert for loose children and peacocks meandering about. Parking is not permitted inside the zoo.

Immediately after you drive through the gate, look to your left to see the education office **(3)** of the zoo. This inconspicuous adobe style building (originally the toll booth for the Cheyenne Mountain Highway) had a covered drive attached to it where you could take your new Model T Ford through the zoo and beyond for 25 cents. This little building used to be a big deal!

At the top of the zoo, signage will direct you to turn left **(4)** on the first of many switchbacks. The loop straight ahead is off limits to the public but it houses support buildings **(5)** and a unique octagon building that once held the zoo carousel. Interestingly, it is also the location of what was the upper terminal of a second miniature cog train that ran up the road inside the zoo so many years ago. (You can see the original railway bed—now grass or bushes—to the right of the road on your way through the zoo).

The original entrance still stands, hidden in plain sight

If the weather allows, open your sunroof as this ride will provide the opportunity to view mountain scenery above your head. Open your windows on your ascent to hear sounds of the animals and the chimes from the Shrine above. Feel the fresh mountain air. Turn on the map display of your GPS just to watch your icon meander up the winding road. As you know by now, we are all about the experiences of the journey, not just the destination.

An automatic chain link gate **(6)** will open for your vehicle. This gate is meant to keep an escaping animal inside the zoo's boundary, but more importantly it keeps the mountain's native

213

wildlife out of the zoo, although an occasional mule deer has been known to sneak through when a car passes. Wave at the people in the chair lift **(7)** as they pass above your head. They wonder how you have the privilege to be on this mountain road above the zoo. To your left, below the chairlift, you can see some of the small cages originally used in the early version of the zoo. These ancient cube shaped enclosures are no longer accessible to the public in the zoo but can be seen clearly from the chairlift. Obsolete now, their stone and steel wire construction has held up well beyond their usefulness. I'm glad they still exist if only to illustrate how animal care has progressed.

On your right, just before the switchback you can spot the remnants of a man-made bear den **(8)**. The cage is gone but the face of the tiny building and metal door are visible, partially covered by fallen rock. Mr. Penrose wanted his guests to experience the Colorado Mountain wilderness during their brief visit. Imagine seeing a (caged) bear on the way up the road! I suppose the travelers could easily approach the cage and feed it. At the original summit lodge, Penrose had similar cages at each side of the grand staircase leading from the parking lot to the lodge—one displaying another live bear; the other, a bobcat.

This road all the way to the top is seven miles long and has 21 switchback turns. It was showcased in Ripley's Believe It Or Not in 1925 as the most crooked road in the world. (This is Spencer Penrose's ability to promote with the best of them.) This new dirt road was able to claim this title because there are 7.5 miles of road inside a 1.25 mile square map grid. I'm sure that once this was published, there were countries on the other side of the world that said "Nice try, America, be we can beat that," but by that time Spencer had the publicity he sought.

On your drive up the road, Hell Gate is a sight to see! Not really, it's just a small boulder pile with a great name. This is the longest stretch of road between switchbacks, and the right side looks down over the city. Only Hell Gate rises above the road level on the right side. It is unique because it is the only spire of boulders on an otherwise long drop off on this stretch of road.

The interesting object here is the black power pole (9) that is still standing in place next to Hell Gate. This is one of the original 1926 lighted utility poles to the summit. Once again I am impressed that these pieces of history were not removed decades ago. On the hillside above you is another pole in the series. Why is it special? Our dear Mr. Penrose couldn't resist the opportunity to promote this lodge in a way that nobody else would dare to attempt. He drew a line from downtown Colorado Springs to the summit and instructed that the iron power poles be installed in the straight line up the face of the granite mountain. He then proceeded to have 26 street lamps installed at the top of the poles. I am picturing an "Eat at Joes" feel to his idea. Electric lights were still an exciting concept, but this was too much. Not only was there a reflective scar switch-backing up the mountain face during the day, but now a string of lights pointing to the lodge at night.

What the city didn't know at the time was that Mr. Penrose had an aircraft navigation beacon on order but it didn't arrive in time for the grand opening. Two months later, at the top of the string of lights up the hill, the city was treated to a bright light flashing once every 10 seconds. A lens about the size of a trash can lid was rotated by a motor on the scaffolding attached to the highest point on the lodge.

Before the road switches back on itself again, this is a good place to stop **(10)** and look out over the city below and the mountain above. Although this road was built in 1925 it wasn't paved until 1966. This chain link fencing was installed in 1925. I had no idea that chain link fencing has been around that long, but it can be seen in brochures from when the road was new. Inside one of the rooms of the Will Rogers Shrine is a photo of Spencer Penrose's 1937 funeral procession with the fence in the background. When you get the chance, grab the fence and give it a good shake. That's steel, not 1960s aluminum.

The fence posts are repurposed railroad rails marked with dates around 1887. It is sheer speculation on our part that they came from Pikes Peak's cog railway. The Pikes Peak and Manitou Cog Railway was built in 1889 and purchased by Spencer Penrose in 1925, the exact same year that this road was built. These rails are buried three fourths underground and one fourth above. It makes us feel better on the drive knowing how sturdy they are.

On the many hikes that I have led over the years, people will marvel that these boulders appear to have been stacked up, and they are right, they are stacked. These stacked rocks have ridden down the eroding mountains over time, stacked by Mother Nature onto the boulders below. Rolling boulders are a common occurrence in the Rockies and the "Watch For Rocks" signs you see on all the public highways all too often have proof lying in the road.

At the end of this switchback, notice how the granite appears different than the rest of the stone on the mountain. Geologists speculate that this set of Rocky Mountains is actually the third version. The two versions that existed before, known as the Ancestral Rockies, disappeared and reappeared through eons of erosion and upheaval. You are on the third version of the mountain range that is about halfway through its erosion process. Try to picture these mountains 3,000 feet higher if you can! The granite at the end of this switchback (still **10)** is different than the lighter and brighter stone you see on the mountain. This switchback is made up of the crumbly yellowish-brown granite remnant of the Ancestral Rockies.

Around the next switchback you will spot a small road **(11)** leading to a set of towers. The face of this mountain was once sprinkled with early radio and TV antennae. This very short spur of a road leading to modern cell equipment is a perfect example of one of these locations. Each radio station had their individual antenna location. The advantage of the extra elevation gave broad coverage to the valley below, but as television signals became more powerful, all of the little antenna towers were combined into one location on the summit of Cheyenne

Mountain. This higher location also solved the problem of coverage to all of southern Colorado because from the summit the view extends almost to New Mexico. Most little antenna locations are little more than abandoned cement slabs in the trees now.

The small roadside sign for Sheercliff Loop **(12)** has been around a very long time and is the last of the original signage. You are entering the Shrine's parking lot. Watch your speed as you pass through the stone and iron gates. Expect to encounter mammals crossing the road while taking selfies on the way to and from the hike to the Shrine.

You have reached the end of the trail at the Will Rogers Shrine's parking lot. At the top of the parking lot is a small shelter with picnic tables and another switchback as the road continues. Beyond this gate **(13)** is the private, gated road to Broadmoor's Cloud Camp.
(www.broadmoor.com/cloud-camp).

Although there are 16 more switchbacks of dirt road beyond the Shrine's parking lot, the remaining road is not open to the public.

Park here and visit the small building next to the entrance gate for historical information and to see the original diorama for the construction of the monument. The restrooms are in the basement.

At the Will Rogers Shrine of the Sun **(14)** you are over 1,000 feet higher than Colorado Springs. This book is about hiking and trailside finds of historic tidbits, but you have been driving. Happily it is now it is time to explore. Follow the path a short distance to the base of the Shrine. Climbing the 94 stairs to the top of the Shrine will provide a stretch for your legs and a treat for your eyes. It may also illustrate that oxygen is not as plentiful at this elevation.

The ten impressive sets of iron doors on the Shrine were made in England specifically for this tower. The five stories of stairs will take you past rooms with murals telling the history of the Pikes Peak Region. Views, murals and historic photographs take you away. The stairs will terminate with breathtaking vistas from the tiny open air rooftop deck. Look up at the flag from this little platform to be introduced to the vertigo that you have been avoiding until now.

Spencer Penrose, the legendary founder of the Broadmoor Hotel and a premier name in the history of Cripple Creek and Colorado Springs built his Penrose Mausoleum on a prominent point on the side of Cheyenne Mountain. During construction, his wife gently suggested that it would be inappropriate to name a structure this grandiose looming over the city after themselves and the wise husband listened. The name was changed to "The Shrine of the Sun". During construction, their acquaintance, Will Rogers, perished in an Alaskan plane crash. Never one to pass up an opportunity for public interest, Spencer Penrose changed the name to The Will Rogers Shrine of the Sun and a bust of Will Rogers was commissioned to be placed on the walkway leading the Shrine. Note that the murals inside are all about the growth of the city. No depiction of Mr. Rogers. He has a few photographs on display on the floors above and he is buried in the Forest Lawn Cemetery in California. You may visit the small chapel in the basement where the Spencer and Julie Penrose are interred along with two friends and business associates from his early days. Why were these two other individuals so special? They were investors in Spencer's operations, but more importantly, one was the champion player on Spencer's beloved polo team. The other was the captain. Will Rogers also put his horsemanship on display as a pretty good polo player and there is even a Will Rogers Polo Club still in operation in Pacific Palisades, California.

In the base of the Shrine is a room of chimes with the east wall opening to the valley below. You can't explore in front of the chimes due to the volume but you can easily and safely walk on top of the room. Westminster style chimes in the Shrine can be heard for miles on the plains below. In the stillness of the mountain, feel the breeze and listen for a primate's howl or a peacock's cry. If you are lucky a lion's roar will be carried up from far below.

Will Rogers Shrine's Curator, George, pointed out that the granite for this shrine was quarried from a single boulder near the switchback that you can see on the ridge above. This assured that the color and texture of the stones matched exactly. This magnificent 114-ft tower was built of iron, cement and granite. No nails or wood were used. Outside the eastern base of the tower, there is a series of brass plaques that denote points of interest below. We love the fact that four of them are outdated by decades. My favorite is "Corley Mountain Highway," now named the Gold Camp Road. It hasn't been called Corley Mountain Highway for 80 years. The airport plaque points to a location long gone. The Ice Arena and Rodeo Arena plaques point to buildings removed to build the Broadmoor West building across the lake from the original hotel. It's hard to imagine, but 11 early NFL games were hosted in that rodeo arena in the early 20th century. The rodeo arena was carefully moved and is still hosting rodeos as the Norris Penrose event center.

Once you leave the mountain, we suggest a stop at the Penrose Heritage Museum across the street from the Broadmoor Hotel. It is free to the public, but parking in the adjacent garage is not. This pristine museum has made use of its prime space to the maximum effect. Did we mention it's free? The curator and team are most anxious to tell you the stories and show off the artifacts. Julie and Spencer Penrose's carriages are on display with other artifacts. The other half of the museum tells the stories and showcases cars through the years from the annual Pikes Peak Hill Climb, displayed on a unique inclined ramp representing the Pikes Peak Highway on its most exciting day of the year.

Next door to the museum, inside the building to the right (over the parking garage) is a large reproduction of a pen-and-ink brochure about the highway above the zoo. There are displays and photographs in the Colorado Hall. If there are no events going on you are welcome to admire this little bonus. Behind this building is the World Figure Skating Museum and Hall of Fame.

As long as you're here, why not walk around the hotel's lake? It is one more opportunity to admire the architecture and history that is Spencer and Julie Penrose and to hear the Will Rogers Shrine chimes emanating from the hillside above.

A Step Farther:
The Mountaineer's final stop

You gotta love tiny trains. I sure do; always have. Not the vintage Lionel model train sets, track and little tabletop villages with miniature mountain tunnels, but small trains that people can ride with open boxcar seating.

When I was young my parents would take us kids to a drive-in theater in Southern California that had a full children's playground under the huge outdoor screen. This place also had a small train that would transport the children in a large oval around the base of the screen, and to imaginary travel destinations far beyond—until dusk when the dancing and singing popcorn containers and soft drinks appeared on the movie screen as concession-sirens directing guests to the snack bar. When I moved to Colorado with my family, I took my young kids to the Tiny Town Railroad in Morrison. I presume they enjoyed it as much as I did when the tiny train took us around all the tiny stores, tiny houses, tiny trees and tiny parks, tooting its tiny train horn.

So, you might understand my pleasure at discovering the restored historic remains of the miniature cog train that ran from the Broadmoor Hotel lake to the Cheyenne Mountain Zoo. The futuristic-looking little train, named the Mountaineer, made round trips every hour and was a real favorite of zoo visitors. The train engine and passenger cars were designed and built by the GM/Cadillac Company, and powered by a V-8 motor. The sleek train engine pushed two covered coaches (each seating 20 visitors) up the grade, and then traveled back down holding the cars behind.

Most might entirely miss this little find, unless you were looking for it. Today, the fully-restored white train engine is located at the south end of the zoo's parking lot, by the zoo's entrance pillars. The engine sits on a piece of the original track and you can also see that sections of the cog rails are used around the parking lot as barriers.

I walked around the engine that looked like it had been imported from Disneyland's Tomorrowland attraction, ran my hand across the refurbished smooth enamel paint, and peered inside the windows at the controls. How I would have loved to have ridden the train from the hotel past the golf course and then the thick scrub oak and spruce forest, seeing squirrels and deer scramble at the rumble as the passengers traveled in and out of four tunnels on the way to the zoo. The sound of the engine, as well as the breeze blowing the smell of pine trees into the open cars, would have been mesmerizing to me.

The Cadillac powered cog engine on display

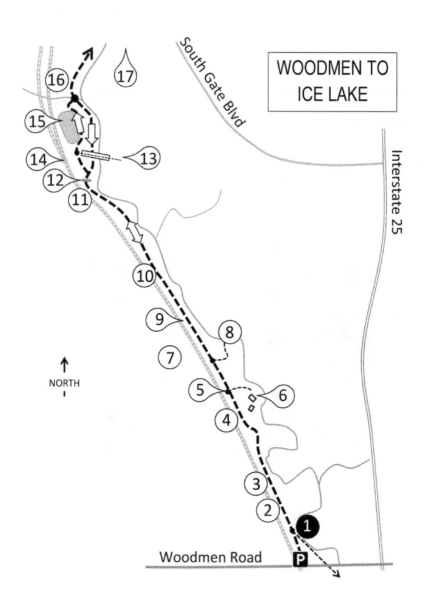

WOODMEN TO
ICE LAKE

17

South Gate Blvd

Interstate 25

16

15

14

13

12

11

10

9

8

7

5

6

NORTH

4

3

2

1

Woodmen Road

P

19
Woodmen to Ice Lake

A trail so good it has four names

The Pikes Peak Greenway Trail runs through town paralleling Monument Creek. For many years this trail ended at gated private land. The New Santa Fe Trail ran from Palmer Lake through the US Air Force Academy and ended nearby at the other side of the private property. In 2000, the city was finally able to obtain the land and connect the two trails. A "golden" spike was driven and the mayor's speech jokingly compared this link of the two trails to the meeting of the transcontinental railroad. This connection was doubly important as these two trails are also part of the 876-mile Colorado Front Range Trail that will someday span from Wyoming to New Mexico. Many pieces are in place, just waiting for connections such as this.

This 2.5 mile trail is wide and mostly level. Keeping in mind that the first word of this book's title is "Easy," we rated the trail a moderate because it has some undulations into gullies with snow and ice in the winter shadows. During the summer months it can be muddy as the soil is not the decomposed granite that we enjoy on so many hikes. This mud dries to preserve the imprint of hiking boots, bike tires, dog paws and hoof prints.

The New Santa Fe Trail enters the United States Air Force Academy and may be closed at the boundary under certain circumstances.

Getting there: From Interstate 25, take Woodmen Road, exit 149, west for one quarter mile. Immediately after crossing the bridge over the creek, turn right into the Edmondson Trailhead parking lot.

The Hike: From the parking lot, take the trail to the north, paralleling the railroad tracks. Just below the parking lot, continue straight ahead at the junction of another trail. The trail to the right that cuts back **(1)** underneath Woodmen Road goes to downtown Colorado Springs and Monument Valley Park.

Distance: 5 Miles

Difficulty: 🌲🌲🌲🌲🌲

Elevation Gain: 100 feet

Mile marker 38.5 **(2)** illustrates our location on the Pikes Peak Greenway Trail. Silhouetted up on the hill to your left is the gate to the private property that once blocked the connection **(3)**, still entwined with the original barbed wire and a combination lock. The gate's original location was near the trail split below the parking lot and moved to this hill in celebration.

A bit farther down the road is mile marker 39 **(4)**. That was a quick half mile, wasn't it? Mile marker 39 shows the Pikes Peak Greenway logo on one side and the New Santa Fe Trail on the other.

The previously unpopular gate, still padlocked

When the trail passes into a treeless area, look to your right for the remains of a stone building near the creek. There is a narrow trail through the grasses **(5)** that will take you to the remnants of two old stone buildings **(6)**. Take a moment to examine how these stones are laid as the stonework on these two buildings is quite unique. Although most stones are rusted sedimentary found nearby, there are a few stones that appear to have been brought in. There is also a cut block of sandstone.

I was informed by a friend of the family that lived in this area that these two buildings are the remnants of a stage coach stop. Quite an exciting discovery, but I doubted that is was a stage stop at first, because it is on the wrong side of the creek as

227

the road between Denver and Colorado Springs. Upon research, I discovered that the original road ran between Denver and Old Colorado City, not Colorado Springs. This first Denver Road ran through the foothills where the Air Force Academy is now. It roughly followed Rockrimmon Blvd, then along Garden of the Gods Road area and down near 30th Street, ending at 28th and Colorado Ave. This route would have placed the first road on this side of the river and right through this area. Eureka, maybe! I also found documentation that these buildings were already in ruins before 1947.

Stage stop stonework

Back on the main trail; look for a gate **(7)** in the fence on your left. The gate still stands framed by railroad ties for fence posts but the road no longer exists. Old maps show this rough road accessing the bluffs to the west. Above this gate and to the right, is a perfect example of some hoo-doos, limestone boulders on top of their thin pedestals.

228

On the right side of the main trail, spot a narrow trail leading off to the right **(8)**. It will quickly turn left and through a cut down the hill. This trail leads to a narrow gate of two vertical iron pipes. The fallen gate lies in the weeds nearby. Use caution in this area as there is a cattle guard hidden in the grasses to the left of the opening with no sign of the road that it once protected. Do not proceed beyond this fence line. Return back to the main trail and turn right to continue the exploration.

On your left is the railroad spike driven into a boulder **(9)** accompanied by a brass plaque commemorating the connection of the Pikes Peak Greenway and the New Santa Fe Trail.

Look under the stone culvert **(10)** to your left. Sturdy rectangles of stone, these pieces of handy work from the 19th century are a reminder that although there was a rush to build the railroads, care had to be taken that the rails would stay in place. It apparently was also important that they look good, even though this was a distance outside of town at the time.

Not far from the 40-mile marker is a large piece of railroad iron. This was the grease box and axel mount assembly for a train car. This heavy cast iron piece appears to have been torn apart. There is a 1918 date casting in the iron.

Fountain Creek has a history of flooding. This tight bend in the river must have sparked some emergency erosion prevention action at one time. On your left you will discover eight railroad flat cars **(11)** used to reinforce the banks of the railroad track. A date of 1940 is cast in one of the iron couplings. On your right are some railroad rails anchored with heavy cable on the bank of the creek. Behind one of the flat cars, the sporty racing stripe on a blue Dodge DART Swinger's rear fender can be seen peeking out of the debris.

As you approach the United States Air Force Academy's property, many signs and a fence **(12)** make it quite clear that you are entering a US Air Force installation. Still, it is much more low key that the checkpoints that are encountered when driving in.

You will know when the trail enters the US Air Force Academy

Not too much farther, you will encounter an intersection in the trail. Take the left fork to access the lake. Your return route will bring you back under the foot bridge **(13)** over the trail.

On the railroad tracks to your left is a grand collection of silver-colored communication, switching and signaling equipment **(14)** for a siding.

Ice Lake **(15)** was here long before the Academy. When the Academy was built in mid-1950s, a small town and several ranches were removed. At Ice Lake, follow the trail around to the other side. Just beyond the lake are some active beaver dams **(16)**. Turn right and follow the trail under the foot bridge to return on the trail you came in on. Underneath this footbridge are massive support columns for the train bridge that once stood in this exact same place.

If you desire a longer hike, turn left. The trail continues (17) to follow Monument Creek all the way through the Academy and beyond—all a continuing beautiful trek. Within one half mile of the lake, a cube shaped house is seen across the creek. This home from an earlier time was one of the few buildings spared when the Academy was built. One mile from the lake, the trail will cross underneath Southgate Boulevard. Look up for the mud nests of Cliff Swallows built underneath the bridge.

You can have a similar hiking experience by starting at the trailhead next to the Air Force Academy's North Gate entrance.

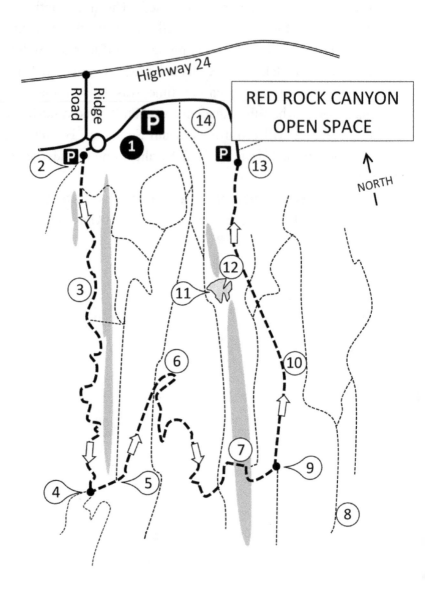

20

Red Rock Canyon

The Garden of the Goddesses

The Red Rock Canyon Open Space is a southern extension of the Garden of the Gods Park and can be easily accessed on the south side of Highway 24. The Open Space trail system can get busy on the weekends, yet less crowded than Garden of the Gods. Red Rock Canyon has plenty of parking and the varieties of formations are easily accessed.

Nearby, the Garden of the Gods Park is a treasure. It has huge pristine sandstone spires framing Pikes Peak and this post card scenery is a big part of what makes the area such a tourist mecca. Garden of the Gods was voted by Trip Advisor in 2014 as the best city park in the nation. I'm sure that the Golden Gate Park in San Francisco and New York's Central Park were green with envy. (Pun intended.) The park remains in the top ten best attractions.

Here's an idea: let's cut up the Kissing Camels rock formation in Garden of the Gods into red sandstone blocks to make buildings for our beautiful town and ship even more to Denver. We could also fill in the valley between the majestic ridges of red sandstone with a city dump. There is even a nice flat spot at the base of the rocks to put a trailer park. Now that's what we call big city progress. Woo-hoo!

As hard as it is to imagine in today's world, that is exactly what was done in Red Rock Canyon. While Garden of the Gods was given to the city to be protected as a city park in 1909, the formations to the south were privately owned and used as a quarry and garbage dump. The Red Rock Canyon was purchased from the private owners in 2003 and the city has opened up the sandstone quarry with trails that explore the workings of the past. Two adjacent properties were also purchased making it a 1,400-acre park with 30 miles of intersecting trails. Holy cow, that's a lot of trails for us to explore and enjoy.

This park is one of our favorite places to lead guided hikes because of the mix of manmade history and unique natural features, not to mention a wide variety of trial types. (www.redrockcanyonopenspace.org)

The city dump has been covered over and is being reclaimed. The quarry's buildings and equipment are long gone, leaving only the carved-up sandstone fins for evidence. The trailer park has been removed and converted into a second parking lot for the Red Rock Canyon Open Space.

The route for this hike will only cover a very small portion of the whole park. We encourage you to explore more of the park another time. The trails in this chapter were chosen to highlight a variety of interesting points, but there is so much more to Red Rock Canyon Open Space for your future visits. We will be hiking up the Contemplative Trail, then connecting to the Quarry Pass Trail, and finally returning on the Red Rock Canyon Trail back down to the parking lot. The three legs of the hike are each approximately one mile long. Although the trails are in great shape, there are some elevation ups and downs and some boulders to navigate across.

Hiking, biking, trail running, horseback riding, dog loops, rock climbing and even paragliding are official activities in this park. There are no restrooms inside the park, only at the parking lots. The Colorado Springs Parks, Recreation & Cultural Services states: "It is easier to climb up than to climb down. Save yourself from a dangerous predicament by staying on the ground. Technical climbers are required to register at the Garden of the Gods Visitor Center. Technical Climbing is permitted in groups of two or more with proper climbing equipment. All other climbing over 10 feet off the ground is illegal, and may result in a fine of up to $500 and/or 90 days in jail." Tempting, but understood.

Getting there: From Colorado Springs, head west on Highway 24. Turn left on Ridge Road which is the last intersection before reaching Manitou Springs. Continue through the roundabout to the left and park in the large parking lot.

The hike: The first point of interest that you will spot is the exposed layers **(1)** of earth next to the parking lot. This is what the ground under our feet looked like before it was stood on end by the rising Rocky Mountains. Note that all the upheaval on the Front Range leans towards the mountains.

From the parking lot, walk back to the roundabout that you just navigated when you came in. Just as you enter the smaller parking lot, turn left, south on a narrow dirt trail that heads towards the ridge of stone **(2)** nearby. Do not take the road width trail into the flat area. You will be on Sand Canyon Trail to begin with and then on Contemplative Trail that follows along the right side of this ridge all the way. When you come to an intersection in the trail, (underneath the power lines) follow the trail straight ahead between the stone ridges. This is the start of the Contemplative Trail.

The Contemplative Trail was built by a free spirited group of locals that supported the naming of the park as The Garden of the Goddesses when it was purchased by the city. Had they succeeded, that may have been a better name, as there are numerous locations around the state and country with the Red Rock name. The Red Rock Amphitheatre west of Denver is in Red Rock Park. We will be hiking another Red Rock above Woodland Park in this book. Arguably, the most famous is the massive 195,000-acre Red Rock Canyon national conservancy area near Las Vegas, Nevada.

The Contemplative Trail will split and rejoin a couple of times, but don't worry—as long as you keep the stone ridge close on your left, you are heading in the right direction. This gradual uphill trail provides numerous places to pause, explore, scramble, hide and contemplate. By design, only hiking is permitted on this particular trail so that your contemplation is not interrupted by mountain bikes. Rustic log benches **(3)** are found in select areas along this particular trail. One bench has a small plaque referencing the creative Garden of the Goddesses group. Take your time to enjoy this strip of tranquility in nature, as we will soon encounter a massive example of man's touch on the park.

At the top of the trail **(4)** you will encounter a marked junction with several options. To the right will take you to Manitou Springs or straight ahead will take you to the Roundup Trail which is a bit more challenging with more elevation gain. Straight ahead would also connect to the Section 16 Trail and Ring the Peak trails. We are headed for the Quarry, so turn left on the Quarry Pass Trail. You will encounter a fork almost immediately. Avoid the sharp left that goes north **(5)** back along the other side of the ridge, and stay on the Quarry Pass Trail.

As you head for the rock quarry, this trail will intersect two wide, road-like trails running up the hill. Cross over these trails and continue on the single track that you are on. Watch for the point where the view quickly opens up **(6)** and Garden of the Gods pops into view. This is a good spot to pause and take in your location. You can see how the ridges of Red Rock Canyon continue as Garden of the Gods. By the way, there are Red Rock Trails in Boulder and Denver, too.

Soon you will get your first view of the quarry **(7)**. Look through a break in the ridge to the right of the quarry to see a large semi-flat grassy meadow **(8)** with pipes protruding from it. This is 62 acres of city dump in the process of reclamation. On

Stairs carved for the quarry worker's access

the shale and limestone ridges beyond the dump are the prehistoric fossils of the past and another parking area to access Red Rock Canyon Open Space. There are so many hiking trail options in this park that will keep you coming back again and again.

Your trail will drop down to the base of the sandstone ridge with the quarry. Once you reach the ridge, ascend into the quarry and explore. You will be exiting out the other side of the quarry. Take your time to study the quarry's edges and corners and marvel at how they could cut and move the 6' x 6' x 10' blocks of stone using 19th century technology. Notice the flat vertical cuts, but rough bottoms? They had a steam driven machine that would chip away to cut the sides. Then they would drill a horizontal hole where the bottom would be and place one to two pounds of black powder to blast the bottom loose. There were three different companies harvesting stone in this area at the same time. From 1888 to 1902 this was quite a business. Around the start of the 1900s, steel and concrete construction took over and the artistic sandstone carved facades faded in popularity. The sandstone from this quarry built many of Denver's nicer buildings, as well as a key bank building in Downtown Colorado Springs (see **A Step Farther** below).

Exit the quarry on the opposite side that you entered. As you descend into the valley floor, note the stairs carved for the stone worker's access in several places. Keep looking, as there are actually three different sets of narrow steps that can be spotted on this side of the ridge. Continue across the narrow valley to the dirt road **(9)** running parallel to the next ridge. The interpretative signs give you more information on the sandstone quarry's operation.

Turn left on Red Rock Canyon Trail and head downhill. This was the original rail bed to the quarry. As you head back down, keep your eyes open for rock climbers **(10)** on both sides of the valley. In the outfitting company that I guided for, we said that those on the sides of the cliffs were the rock-climbers and our groups were jokingly called the dirt-walkers. I'm okay with that—I prefer my boots on the ground.

At the top of the ridge on your left, look for two exploratory vertical cuts that could have been a start to the next quarry. On your right, notice the ripples in the stone that were once sand dunes.

The lake on your left **(11)** was built by the Bock family that purchased the closed quarries. Mr. Bock's brick house was creatively converted into the open-air pavilion **(12)** for the park. The level area between the home and lake held a modern

Pond near the open-air pavilion

swimming pool. The rock wall on the other side of the road was a string of garages and a hidden Cold War bomb shelter of five-foot thick concrete walls. His plan was to have condominiums, business centers and a golf course built on this land. It would have been an interesting location, but we can all be thankful that the people of Colorado Springs were able to add this land to the collection of exceptional parklands within the city limits.

Once you hit the parking lot you can appreciate what a nice flat location they chose for a mobile home park. There was some quarry activity quite close to the parking lot. Notice that the cuts are different, and smaller, than the quarry that you passed through earlier. These sandstone blocks were mined by a different company. From the parking lot, you will notice a trail cutting through the hillside **(13)** heading uphill to your right. This will connect with the eastern half of the park that could very well be your next exploration. To return to your starting point, follow the road past the free-ride bicycle area back **(14)** to the large parking lot.

We just took you through one small trail of a much larger park. Come back and explore when you can. There is another parking lot and entrance on 31st Street near Rudy's BBQ. A third entrance and parking lot on 26th Street was the original gate and road to the city dump that fills the valley in the park.

The damage to this park will never be hidden, and it shouldn't be. It may be hard to witness, but it tells a story of the city's early years. On the bright side, the trails will never be as crowded as the park's larger and more famous counterpart.

A Step Farther:
Chunks of history

Have you ever wondered what some of the cut rocks from the sandstone quarry were used for, or what they looked like when given a decorative and utilitarian purpose? On your drive west to Red Rock Canyon, from Downtown Colorado Springs, not far from the I-25 interchange, on Highway 24 westbound, you will encounter something significant on your left—a little tough to see as you drive by in moving traffic and nowhere really to park to get out for exploring.

As you get close to 8th Street, observe (still keeping your eyes on the road) quite a collection of large, carved sandstones. These are pieces of the ornate, First National Bank, once an impressive building in downtown Colorado Springs, that were uncovered recently with road construction, the rubble of the building was used as road fill. Can you imagine?

Of all the things we did right through the years, demolishing the First National Bank in June of 1955 was not one on them. This beautiful building once stood on the northwest corner of Tejon Street and Pikes Peak Avenue, constructed in 1894 with an Italian Renaissance style interior and floors made of Tennessee marble. The bank was called "the finest and best banking quarters in the West." The building would certainly have stories to tell through the years from the Colorado Gold Rush to the Great Depression, and all along the way, customers and pedestrians would have been able to have enjoyed the sandstone embellishments on the exterior. But not all was lost. In 2016, the Colorado Springs Pioneers Museum accepted a donation of 25,000 pounds of capital stone originally part of the 1894 building.

Back to our unearthed chunks of history: Some of the intricately carved façade blocks and slabs can be seen on display today on your drive to or from this exploration, reintroduced remnants from times gone by. Some of these blocks weighing hundreds to thousands of pounds were dug up unexpectedly by construction crews near Fountain Creek and Highway 24, the "rock" originally used as fill at the construction of this exchange in the 1950s when the bank building was torn down. Out of the ground it came, and back into the ground it went. Surprisingly, when it was discovered again, much of the carved stone was in pretty good shape. About 36 of these relics can be seen near 8th Street on the newly-built section to direct traffic flow. A bit of historic downtown is still on display. That rocks!

Remnants of carved sandstone columns on display

Preparation and Building a Responsible Daypack
The Eight Essentials

Most of the hikes and explorations in this book are relatively easy with moderate round-trip mileage and well-marked trails. The question might be asked, "Why would I need a daypack, and why should I stuff these items in it for such short hikes?" The simple answer is you may never need all of the Eight Essentials, but why not have them anyway, just in case. The list below is not only good recommendations for our local hikes, but for any treks on which you may embark.

A good portion of the adventures in this book will take you to wilderness areas, so you should be prepared for any possible situation you may encounter. Should something unexpected happen—anything from tripping on a tree root to being caught in a typical Colorado summer afternoon thunderstorm—wouldn't you want to be ready to be self-sufficient, have the answers/remedy for any surprises, or be in a position to help others as well?

I once came upon a small group of hikers on my way down from summiting a Colorado 14er. Six people stood around a companion who had fallen down on the trail and none of them had a basic first aid kit to help the poor woman suffering from minor cuts and scrapes. I stopped to see if I could be of some assistance, pulling out my first aid bag. I cleaned and dressed her wounds, all to the surprise and appreciation of the hiker and her unprepared onlookers. Another time, I encountered a disheartened gentleman who had gone over his dirt bike handlebars while rock hopping sandstone dunes in Moab. He had dislocated his shoulder as well as acquiring some nasty road rash. Having no first aid of his own, I tended to his injuries and helped him with a sling I had in my pack for his arm. And, I seem to fall down a lot on trails myself ... good for me to at least have a handful of Band-Aids!

ESSENTIALS:
The checklist below is deliberately comprehensive. It includes more items than you'll likely need in the Pikes Peak Region for short treks. You can adapt your pack to what you think is wise for your trip. I tend to carry more items in my pack than others, but at one time or another, I have used everything I've brought with me for one circumstance or another. Better to have more than you think you'll need, whether you use it or not, than to need something and not have it.

1) Appropriate Footwear
Happy feet make for a happy hike. Comfortable, well-fitting footwear is super important. Think about traction, support, and protection, and footwear well suited for the terrain described in these chapter explorations, either hiking boots or trail runners.

2) Water
Stay hydrated, my friend. You may even want to start drinking water on your way to the trailhead parking area. For your hike, as a guideline, plan for a half liter per hour in moderate temperatures. We recommend carrying more water than you think you'll need.

3) Trail Snacks
Bring plenty of calorie-dense foods to help fuel your hike. And like water, pack beyond the minimum expectation in case you

are out longer than planned. You can always take some home and use for your next adventure!

4) First Aid Kit
Have at least the bare minimum of supplies to treat injury or illness. This may sound a bit dramatic given that our hikes in this book are "easy" ones, but this brings us back to the "why not" be prepared. A small bag of these supplies doesn't take up much space, nor add that much extra weight. Understand that having first aid supplies is only as helpful as your knowledge of how to use them. The American Red Cross offers an excellent wilderness first aid and CPR course in the Springs. (https://www.redcross.org/local/colorado/take-a-class/first-aid-colorado-springs-co)

5) Weather-appropriate Clothing
Be sure to check the forecast for the day and dress for the conditions—and remember, the weatherman is not always right. Dress in layers to be able to adjust to changing weather and activities. Consider wearing moisture-wicking items. I like to toss a rain poncho in the pack too, even one of those cheap disposables. And I often bring along a lightweight jacket, windbreaker or fleece.

6) Safety Items
Have a flashlight or headlamp and a whistle at a minimum. With these items you have the ability to see the trail and your map in the dark, should that be necessary (let's hope not!) or whistle for help.

7) Map and Compass

Cell phones and GPS units are handy tools, but they are not always reliable in a wilderness setting. We've provided detailed and descriptive maps to these trials—take the book with you, cut the maps out, or photocopy pages for your explorations.

8) Sun Protection

The air is very thin at the elevation of the Pikes Peak Region. Sunscreen, sunglasses, and sun-protective clothing (long-sleeve shirt, cap or broad brimmed hat) are recommended for every season of the year in Colorado, regardless of temperature or cloud cover.

PLUS A FEW MORE:

Depending on the particulars of the hike and on expected weather conditions, there are a few more items you may want to bring with you.

o Gloves or mittens
o Knife or multi-tool
o Rainwear (jacket and pants)
o Hiking stick
o Knit beanie cap or balaclava
o Camera
o ID
o Change of clothing/shoes in car
—TDJ

Trail rules

Of course, we are all familiar with the wilderness trial hiking rule, "Leave no trace." Pack out what you brought in with you (even what you think are biodegradables), be gentle on the path, don't leave your initials on a tree or boulder for the next 100 years. (I don't even like the unnecessary additional cairns or artsy rock sculptures left by others—nearly as bad as graffiti.) This all makes sense—you want to leave the natural environment as pristine as you found it (hopefully) for the next adventurer.

But there are other rules and trail etiquettes that the responsible hiker will want to observe. Most of these may seem obvious to you, but they bear repeating, even for the experienced explorer.

□ Stay on the designated trail. Assume the trail system was designed for a purpose, whether for clear direction, safety, ease, protection of the environment, respect of private property, etc. And short-cuts are rarely worth the effort.

□ Stay to the right on wider paths; pass on the left. When overtaking someone, let them know you are approaching on their left.

□ If you expect other hikers on the trail, when you stop for a view, a rest, or to yield, move off the trail to a durable spot so it is free for others, perhaps those with a faster pace. Commonly used trail sharing rules are: Bikers yield to hikers and horses; hikers yield to horses. You are in no hurry—take the time to yield the trail for a short rest and to wave and say "hello" to those who pass.

☐ Know the rules, the trail or wilderness guidelines specific to the area/region you are hiking in, for example, a National Forrest area. Respect fences and boundary lines.

☐ Leave your loud cell phone talking, or music on speakers, back in the urban area. I like the quiet of the forest, the chirping of birds, and the barking of squirrels over the sounds that remind me of the civilization I trying to escape. If you simply must have your music, consider others and bring you ear buds.

☐ Take a photo out with you, but not pretty rocks or a floral bouquet of wildflowers.

☐ Most of the hikes in this book are not so long that you can't "hold it" until you get back to any convenient restroom not far from your car. But if you have to "go," get waaaay off trail (never near a water source), dig a cat hole, bury and spread leaves and pine needles. Conventional advice has been to bag and carry out TP, but many are saying today that it's okay to have TP go underground now, as it decomposes quickly.

☐ Clean up after your pup. And this doesn't just mean bagging the business and setting it to the side of the trail (what ... for someone else to pick up?). Yeah, apparently, that's a thing.

☐ Be friendly—a "howdy" with a smile and a wave goes a long way. We are all here for the same great experiences. You won't be surprised by the cordial response in return.—TDJ

Hiking with your senses

"Let's stop here for a moment. What do you hear?" After a moment of puzzled silence, the responses are typically "I don't hear anything," "A bird" or "The breeze in the trees?" giving a question in response. There are so many sounds that are overlooked because we are listening too hard.

Try again. Your heart pounding in your ears after a strenuous part of the trail. Your hiking partner's heavy breathing. Traffic in the extreme distance. An airplane's power echoing from the mountains somewhere far away. A rustle of leaves from critters nearby. You hear the crunching of the trail underfoot.

The winds come in waves from the tall mountains behind. Pausing to listen from the crest of a ridge, the aspen leaves will rustle in the valley below. Then the leaves will quake and fall on your ridge, followed by the sound of leaves on the opposite valley as the wave passes over. A moment later, the next wave approaches. This is a magical experience that many miss if not seeking natures input.

In my early days as a hiking guide, we had a yoga instructor teach us the art of being in the moment while on a hike. We are good at tuning out our surroundings as our brains wander a different direction than our feet. It is natural to think about life outside of the hike, and a hike in the woods is a perfect place to work out problems, find solutions, or anticipate what you will do after the hike. When you bring yourself back into the present, your senses enrich the experience many times over.

What do you smell? Many hikers know to look (or sniff) beyond the obvious. Dust? Moisture from an approaching rain?

250

Pine trees. OK, good. Try again. Is that you or a nearby hiking partner? Ewww! What else can you smell? That energy bar that you are nibbling on? The musty smell of the forest floor? When hiking through a stand of ponderosa pine, you may be treated to a subtle sweet aroma. If you place your nose into the crevice of the deep bark of a healthy ponderosa pine, you will smell vanilla. Some people smell butterscotch. Either way, everyone comes out with dust on their nose.

The sense of sight is the one that gives the biggest reward on a mountain hike. I have learned that people see differently and that one person's experience can be vastly different the next hiker. It is beneficial to take turns being the lead. The adventure is more real if you aren't just watching the feet of the person in front of you. And may I suggest to you that if you walk quietly, and *listen* intently to the subtle forest noises, you might actually *see* more wilderness critters.

I tend to seek the bigger view and my wife, Stacy, is good at seeing the details. When she alerts me that I almost stepped on a caterpillar or a columbine, it is because I was looking at the ridgeline of the hills ahead or peering down the hillside. When I point out those mountains, she had not noticed them because she was looking at Mother Nature's finer details. We are good for each other that way.

Stop for an extended period of time. Find a comfortable spot to sit. Don't talk, just stare. The longer you can do this the more you will be surprised at the details. You may spot buildings in the distance, power lines, tree damage caused by lighting or a snow slide's path, and birds making the most of the ever present updrafts. One particular tree may have a pile of pinecone bits below a squirrel's favorite dining spot. You will absorb more while sitting still. I was taught something similar while learning to scuba dive. The instructor said that instead of chasing fish to get a picture, on the next dive, put on some extra weights and sit on the ocean floor leaning against a rock for the entire tank. Fish are curious and the residents of the reef will come to you. It was an enlightening experience and I think of it often when sitting in the mountains.

Take time to feel the plants. (Not the poison ivy or oak.) Different subspecies of evergreen trees have vastly different needles. You may be surprised that they are not round. Some are three sided, some are square. How many needles sprout from a single base? Hold a small rock in your hand while you are moving and think about what has that rock experienced over the eons.

Dog sticks are one of my favorite things to point out on a "senses" hike. On busier trails it is fun to spot "the perfect stick". Once you start looking for them you will be surprised how many perfect carrying sticks line the sides of the trail, having been carried back and forth numerous times by countless hiking buddies.—RS

Hiking lessons that I have learned, some the hard way

You would be surprised how flat a peanut butter and jelly sandwich can become if not packed properly. Use M&Ms in your trail mix, not chocolate chips. The heat of the backpack will make a gooey mess of the chocolate chips but when you bring it back to your refrigerator, it will meld your ziplock bag into a tasty chocolate adhesive peanut bar.

Have sandals ready in your car because it feels so good to get those hiking boots off for the drive home. Even if you drive home barefoot, you won't want to put the boots back on when you get home. A protein shake or an electrolyte drink in your cup holder is a welcome sight at the end of the adventure.

When I pause my hike for a snack, I frequently place an offering to the Squirrel Gods with a few nuts on a flat rock as a tradition. When I pass that alter on the way back, the offering is GONE! Spooky, I know, but I believe!

Place your backpack within easy reach for the drive home. A snack and water from your hydration pack will be welcome at the red lights. On my drive home after a successful hike for this book, I reached in my backpack for a snack and felt the shape of an oily circular plastic piece that I could not identify. I would have to check it out when I got home. Because I was driving, I located my snack by feel, and popped the trail mix in my mouth. My lips and tongue were immediately set on fire. It turned out that the plastic piece was the top that had broken off of my 12 year old can of bear spray and I was lucky the whole thing didn't empty into my pack. Don't do that. Moral of the story; take care of your stuff.—RS

Historical research in the Pikes Peak Region

Let's face it, we are fortunate to have a variety of recreation opportunities close at hand, but the remnants of our forefathers don't go back to the Mayflower or Jamestown. Plymouth Rock is recent news compared with the histories that can be traced back thousands of years in Europe.

With the notable exception of the Spanish explorers and Native Americans, our region's human history only stretches back to the intoxicated miners and intrepid settlers of 170 years ago. We get excited when we stumble across a garbage dump of vintage rusty cans.

When you visit a trail, do you ask yourself how it started? What activities led someone to create this path? Do the remnants of a fallen cabin get your curiosity going? Where do you start? I do research before and after a hike. And then probably hike it again.

Start with Google Earth Even social trails can be seen when zooming in on the satellite photographs. This is the best way to find old roadbeds, building foundations in the nearby woods, and mine tailings than you would otherwise pass by. Be sure to check the Terrain check box.

The Historic Aerials website is an amazing tool. You can compare an aerial photograph that was taken 80 years ago directly with a current shot, and several times in between. It is great for research, but also fun to see what your neighborhood looked like in the 1940s.

The Pikes Peak Library District has an enormous collection of local documents. Check out the PPLD Digital Collections of historic photographs online. Much can be found on the computer, but nothing beats going into the old Carnegie

Library, attached to the back of the Penrose Library on Cascade Avenue. The knowledgeable staff is happy to assist you in your search. Fragile maps of every kind from the history of the Pikes Peak Region can get you lost in the details. When I research, I plan on spending an hour, but will park in a public parking garage because I know from experience that I will be there for half of a day. Their city directories will tell you the story of an address or a person. Much of their inventory can be accessed on their website but they have so much more and nothing beats holding the original document. The Denver Public Library also has a collection that encompasses the state and can be accessed from the comfort of your computer chair.

The Colorado Springs Gazette newspaper has their archives digitized and easily searchable. Marshall Sprague's book, ***Newport in the Rockies***, brings to life the start of the Pikes Peak Region. ***The Pikes Peak Atlas*** by Robert Ormes and Robert Hodak is a must.

The El Paso County Tax Assessor's Office has tax records on land in the county, available to view online. It is quite amazing what you can learn through the transactions listed.

Computers and organizations are fine, but the real secret to getting information is to talk to people. That is something we both don't have a problem doing. Others on the trail may have a story to tell or a memory that will enrich your experience.

Oldtimers They have the stories that you won't find in books. They have the little details. Colorado Natives and Semi-Natives have been around long enough to hear the stories and memories from explorations with their predecessors. Their memories are priceless.

Public parks and spaces frequently have a "**Friends of ...** " group. People that live in the area of a trail or park have a personal connection and they have already gleaned information from others, and are usually eager to share with a person who is genuinely interested. These groups can tell you what that iron pipe used to go to that you spotted sticking up in the middle of a field.

Small museums and local history centers are a treasure trove of historical trivia on an area. The staff knows the area, what happened and which cousin owned the dairy. If they can't answer a question, they know someone else that does.

Computers give us access to so much, but it is the people that bring it to life.—RS

Ranger Rocky guiding the way
Photo courtesy of Kit Bernardi, Travel Journalist & Photographer
KitTravels.com

Rocky Shockley is not a nickname; it is his given name. Leaving Oklahoma for Colorado at a young age, he developed a passion and curiosity for hiking and exploring the *rocky* paths of the Pikes Peak Region. He enjoys finding, researching and sharing the overlooked relics that are found on his trail hikes.

Rocky's years of hotel management experience sharpened his communications skills and developed his love of the tourism industry. Telling the stories of the early history of Colorado Springs is a favorite pastime. He prefers trails that have a history, a story, and discoveries to be found along the way.

Rocky's second career is a professional hiking guide with a historical focus in the Pikes Peak region. This is a perfect fit as he has explored the area most of his life. His stories are told with an energy and enthusiasm that showcase his knowledge of historic trails and the pieces of the past found along the way.

Rocky's favorite quote is: "Hike with your senses." Rocky will often encourage others to stop along the way, to absorb the aroma of the pines, listen to the sounds. To pause to feel the geology of the region that both drew and hindered the prospectors and the pioneers.

Rocky regularly chronicles his discoveries in his blog site: Exploring the Lesser Known Pikes Peak Region. (www.6100feet.com)

Tim in his happy place

T. Duren Jones loves hiking wilderness trails. He gets out as often as he can, and enjoys taking friends and family on his explorations. Most of those who have joined—and survived—his adventures still talk to him. He has hiked hundreds of trails in the American West, has summited all of the 54 Colorado 14,000 ft. peaks (now on his second round with his granddaughter), and has trekked the length of the nearly 500 miles of the Colorado Trail's 28 segments from Denver to Durango. Once he's done with one checklist, he on to the next—now exploring for historic remnants through hikes in the Pikes Peak Region and around the state of Colorado.

A former Periodicals Editorial and Art Director, T. Duren Jones (Tim) has worked in marketing, advertising and publishing for more than 30 years. He currently works for the Broadmoor Hotel in Colorado Springs as a Wilderness Driver to the hotel's mountain camp properties (along with caretaking those camps in the winter off-season). Tim is a published author of two trail hiking books, featuring stories from his adventures, *Tales from the Trails*, and *Trail Mix*, both available on Amazon Books and from WordFire Press.

ACKNOWLEDGMENTS
Rocky

A tip of the hat to The Old Timers that took the time to reminisce and the hikers that we have encountered along the way. They provided so much information that cannot be found in the record books.

While leading a historical hike above the incline for educator Stacy Adair, I was jolted with the advice that I should put my experiences on paper before they are lost. This led to my blog. Tim Jones later made the suggestion that I turn that blog into this book. Tim's experience and knowledge in the publishing industry and his companionship on so many hikes kept this project fun.

Kathy Clark's extensive proofreading, frequently on a Jamaican beach, reminded me repeatedly that the automated spelling and grammar check are not foolproof. Thank you to my wife, Stacy Shockley, for her support and the encouragement to keep moving forward on this project. Thanks to my son Jonathan for challenging me on our first incline hike and to my daughter, Emily, who provides daily humor, positivity and a reminder of what is truly important in life.

ACKNOWLEDGMENTS

Tim

I am grateful to friends and family members who have encouraged me on life's journey and even joined me on some wilderness adventures. Most still talk to me, some continue to accompany me on trail hikes, although many don't believe me anymore that the destination is "just around the bend" or "just another half mile."

I've always enjoyed getting out into nature. I was mildly interested stumbling upon a historical relic along the way. But it wasn't until Rocky Shockley introduced me to the fun of his brand of exploration and discovery that I really got excited about hiking combined with the hunt for the hidden past. Now, I can't get enough of learning about the found remnants of man's touch on the settlement of the American West. Rocky has taught me that each concrete slab, each piece of steel rod sticking up, each stone wall has a story behind it. I was privileged to be part of this project.

Special thanks to my wife Diane Jones for her support of every next crazy project I take on, and her understanding of my need to get out in the beauty and serenity of the wilderness.

A Partial Bibliography

This list is quite incomplete but provides some interesting reading on the area.

The Pikes Peak Atlas—Robert Ormes and Robert Hodak
The Cheyenne Mountain Story by William R Conte
Geologic Folio Red Rock Canyon Open Space by Ken Weissenburger, Sharon Milito and Don Ellis
The History of Pike National Forest—Stories passed down
A history of the Monument Nursery—RG Colwell 1944 In PPLD special collections
Disasters of the Pikes Peak Region—Dennis Daily
Monument Fire Center A Place in History—PPLD Special Collections
The Parks of Colorado Springs—Nancy Lewis
Newport in the Rockies—Marshall Sprague
Money Mountain—Marshall Sprague
A Pikes Peak Partnership, The Penroses and the Tutts—Thomas J Noel and Cathleen M Norman
Fate of a Fairy—Ellen Captain Jack
Our New Road—Bits of Travel at Home (1878)—Helen Hunt Jackson
Ute Indian Prayer Trees of the Pikes Peak Region—John Wesley Anderson